COLOR
AND COLOR PERCEPTION

A STUDY
IN ANTHROPOCENTRIC REALISM

CSLI
Lecture Notes
Number 9

COLOR
AND COLOR PERCEPTION

A STUDY
IN ANTHROPOCENTRIC REALISM

David R. Hilbert

CENTER FOR THE STUDY
OF LANGUAGE
AND INFORMATION

CSLI was founded early in 1983 by researchers from Stanford University, SRI International, and Xerox PARC to further research and development of integrated theories of language, information, and computation. CSLI headquarters and the publication offices are located at the Stanford site.

CSLI/SRI International
333 Ravenswood Avenue
Menlo Park, CA 94025

CSLI/Stanford
Ventura Hall
Stanford, CA 94305

CSLI/Xerox PARC
3333 Coyote Hill Road
Palo Alto 94305

Library of Congress Cataloging-in-Publication Data
Hilbert, David R., 1959–
     Color and color perception.

     (CSLI lecture notes ; no. 9)
     Bibliography: p.
     1. Color – Psychological aspects. 2. Color vision.
I. Stanford University. Center for the Study of
Language and Information. II. Title. III. Series.
BF789.C7H55 1987   152.1'45   87–27643
ISBN 0–937073–15–6
ISBN 0–937073–16–4 (pbk.)

Printed in the United States

To Katie

CONTENTS

ACKNOWLEDGEMENTS

I WISH TO thank the several institutions whose support over the years has made this work possible. In addition to receiving support from Stanford University and the Stanford Philosophy Department, I have been assisted by the Lurcy Foundation, the Sloan Foundation, and the Center for the Study of Language and Information at Stanford University. Without their generous help my work would not have been possible.

John Perry has suffered through more than one project with me and has contributed greatly not only to this work but to my understanding of philosophy in general. In addition, John Dupré and Michael Bratman have also provided invaluable assistance with this project and with others.

My former officemates, Ian Mason and Ludo Peferoen, have provided me with both with friendship and encouragement.

I also thank my parents, Kathryn Dierstein and Roger Hilbert, for their support throughout a long education.

My wife, Katie, has been an active collaborator throughout this project, and it could not have been completed without her assistance. This is as much her achievment as it is mine.

1

CONCEPTIONS OF COLOR

IF ONE LOOKS through the writings of psychologists and other scientists for their views on the ontological status of color, one is likely to find the claim that colors are properties of the brain or central nervous system and not of physical objects. Semir Zeki, one of the leading researchers on the coding of colors in the brain, claims that "The nervous system, rather than analyze colours, takes what information there is in the external environment . . . and transforms that information to construct colours, using its own algorithms to do so. In other words, it constructs something which is a property of the brain, not the world outside."[1] The claim that colors are properties of the nervous system and not of external objects has represented the view of a significant number of researchers in the psychology and physiology of color vision. Although not many philosophers would be willing to adopt such an obviously problematic analysis without qualification, some philosophers have made claims that are similar in important respects. In Frank Jackson's account of color there are two important facts about color, namely:

1. "Colour is not a property of material things," and

2. "Colour is subjective in that it qualifies mental items."[2]

Jackson's account resembles that of Zeki except that colors are properties of sense-data instead of the brain. In both accounts colors

---

[1]Semir Zeki, "Colour coding in the cerebral cortex: The reaction of cells in monkey visual cortex to wavelengths and colours," *Neuroscience* 9, No. 4 (1983): p. 764.

[2]Frank Jackson, *Perception*, Cambridge: Cambridge University Press, 1977 pp. 128–129.

are not properties of ordinary material things but of items more intimately associated with the minds of human beings.

The ontological status of color is of special interest because color is such an important property. Color is, in Aristotelian terms, the proper object of vision, and vision is the most important of the senses for determining the properties of distant objects. Of the properties objects of experience can appear to possess, color is the most salient. Everything we see is seen as having some color and the colors of objects play an important role in our abilities to visually identify and discriminate them.

Pre-reflective common sense is robustly realist about colors and does not distinguish color from other fundamental properties of external objects such as shape or weight. Our pre-reflective attitude towards colors takes them to be properties of the things they are seen to qualify, in just the same sense as the shape of an object is a property of it. We expect the colors of things to persist through changes in illumination and other changes of viewing situation, just as we expect the shape of an object to be independent of the circumstances of perception. Unlike smells or sounds, colors are almost always perceived to be located on or in the objects they qualify. There is no analog in the case of color to the way in which we sometimes speak of sound as travelling through space. Colors are invariably taken to be properties of seen objects and not of the medium which intervenes between the colored thing and the perceiver.

In the face of this realism, there is a recurring position taken by philosophers and physical scientists that takes color, along with some other sensible qualities, to be subjective in a way that properties such as shape are not. Although the history of the philosophy of color is not my main focus, it will be helpful in discerning the main features of contemporary subjectivism if we look at the views of some of the more prominent historical proponents of subjectivism with respect to color. Subjectivism with respect to color arises very early in the history of philosophy: one of the classic early statements of this sort of view is to be found in Democritus. According to him, it is merely a matter of convention as to whether or not an object is termed hot or cold or assigned a particular color: "By convention sweet, by convention bitter, by convention hot, by convention cold, by convention colour: but in reality atoms and void."[3]
According to Democritus, the world is constituted of collections of

[3]G. S. Kirk, J. E. Raven and M. Schofield, *The Presocratic Philosophers*, Cambridge: Cambridge University Press, 983, p. 410.

atoms which lack most of the properties that we commonly attribute to material things. The atoms of Democritus differ chiefly in shape and position, and their various shapes and arrangements are what account for the appearances given in perception.[4]

Instead of tracing the history of theories of color through antiquity and the medieval era, I will jump to the seventeenth century where an account of the secondary qualities similar in many respects to that of Democritus, becomes predominant. Although the terminology of primary and secondary qualities was not developed until later, a clear expression of the distinction is found in Galileo. In *The Assayer*, Galileo argues for a distinction between those qualities that are properties of body taken by itself and those that arise from the interaction of body with the senses. In a striking anticipation of Locke, Galileo argues that

> Whenever I conceive any material or corporeal substance, I immediately feel the need to think of it as bounded, and as having this or that shape; as being large or small in relation to other things, and in some specific place at any given time; as being in motion or at rest; as touching or not touching some other body; and as being one in number, or few, or many. From these conditions I cannot separate such a substance by any stretch of my imagination. But that it must be white or red, bitter or sweet, noisy or silent, and of sweet or foul odor, my mind does not feel compelled to bring in as necessary accompaniments. Without the senses as our guides, reason or imagination unaided would probably never arrive at qualities like these. Hence I think that tastes, odors, colors, and so on are no more than mere names so far as the object in which we place them is concerned, and that they reside only in the consciousness.[5]

As with Democritus, for Galileo there are a limited number of properties that the fundamental particles of matter possess in themselves, and all the other properties objects may appear to have are the creations of the human mind. Immediately following the passage quoted above Galileo claims as a consequence of his view that "if the living creature were removed, all these qualities would be wiped away and annihilated."[6] This sort of relativity to perceiving creatures is one important way of expressing what the subjectivity of the secondary qualities amounts to.

[4]Ibid., pp. 413–415.
[5]Stillman Drake, *Discoveries and Opinions of Galileo*, Garden City, NY: Doubleday & Company, 1957, p. 274.
[6]Ibid., p. 274.

Galileo published *The Assayer* in 1610. During the second half of the seventeenth century subjectivist accounts of color and the advocacy of a distinction between primary and secondary qualities become quite common. This distinction is most famous from its use by John Locke in the *Essay Concerning Human Understanding*, but he was neither original nor alone in drawing such a distinction. Both Robert Boyle and Newton gave subjectivist accounts of color that predate the *Essay*. Boyle defended essentially the same distinction as Locke in *The Origin of Forms and Qualities* published in 1666. The views of Newton, Locke, and Boyle on the subjective nature of colors are all very similar in spite of the differences between Newton and Boyle on the physics of color and light.

In Boyle's account of the primary-secondary quality distinction, we find many of the same points as in the passage from Galileo quoted above. In Boyle's corpuscalarian philosophy, the ultimate constituents of matter are small particles with a limited number of properties. According to Boyle, "Each of these minute parts or *minima naturalia. . .* must have its determinate *bigness* or *size*, and its own *shape*. And these three, namely *bulk, figure*, and either *motion* or *rest. . .* are the three *primary* and most *catholic moods* or affections of the *insensible* parts of matter, considered *each* of them *apart*."[7] The list of primary qualities is completed by the addition of situation or position, by which Boyle means the spatial relations among the fundamental particles. The primary properties are, according to Boyle, "the affections that belong to a body, as it is considered in itself, without relation to *sensitive* beings or to other natural bodies."[8] Thus, as with Galileo, there is a very small number of properties that external objects have in themselves independently of their interaction with other bodies and perceiving beings.

According to Boyle the other properties of objects are all fundamentally dispositional in nature. These dispositional properties fall into two classes: those that consist in a disposition to cause perceivers to have particular kinds of experiences (the sensible properties) and those that consist in a disposition to cause changes in the sensible properties of other objects. The sensible properties result from:

> There being men in the world, whose organs of sense are contrived in such differing ways that one sensory is fitted to receive impressions

[7]Robert Boyle, "The origins of forms and qualities according to the corpuscular philosophy," in *Selected Philosophical Papers of Robert Boyle*, edited by M. A. Stewart, p. 51.
[8]Ibid., p. 51.

from some, and another from other sorts of external objects or bodies without them. . . the perceptions of these impressions are by men called by several names, as *heat, colour, sound, odour,* and are commonly imagined to proceed from certain distinct and peculiar qualities in the external object which have some resemblance to the ideas their action upon the senses excites in the mind: though indeed all these sensible qualities. . . are but the effects or consequents of the above-mentioned *primary affections* of matter.[9]

In spite of our tendency to attribute them to external objects, the sensible qualities have no existence in objects beyond the dispositions grounded in the primary qualities. The primary qualities are the fundamental properties of body, and "there is in the body to which these sensible qualities are attributed nothing of real and physical but the size, shape and motion or rest, of its component particles, together with that texture of the whole which results in their being contrived as they are."[10] Boyle also draws the same conclusion as Galileo: "If we should conceive all the rest of the universe to be annihilated, except any of these entire and undivided corpuscles . . . it is hard to say what could be attributed to it besides matter, motion (or rest), bulk, and shape."[11] In other words, in the absence of perceiving creatures there would be no secondary qualities.

The view of the nature of secondary qualities given by Galileo and Boyle finds its mature expression in Locke. Locke, like his predecessors, distinguishes between the primary qualities which are those that "are utterly inseparable from body," namely, "Solidity, Extension, Figure, Motion, or Rest, and Number."[12] The secondary qualities "are nothing in the Objects themselves, but Powers to produce various Sensations in us by their *primary Qualities*."[13] As did the earlier writers, Locke maintains not only that the secondary qualities are not among the fundamental properties of matter, but that their existence is derivative from the sorts of sensation that they arouse in human perceivers. Also, like Boyle and Galileo, Locke claims that in the absence of perceivers the secondary qualities would not exist. The primary-secondary quality distinction functions to distinguish those properties which are objective from those which are subjective. According to Locke,

[9]Ibid., p. 51.
[10]Ibid., p. 31.
[11]Ibid., p. 30.
[12]John Locke, *An Essay Concerning Human Understanding*, NY: Oxford University Press, 1975, Bk. II, Chap. VIII, § 9.
[13]Ibid., Bk II, Chap. VIII, § 10.

> The particular *Bulk, Number, Figure, and Motion of the parts of Fire, or Snow, are really in them,* whether any ones Senses Perceive them or no: and therefore they may be called *real Qualities,* because they really exist in those Bodies. But *Light, Heat, Whiteness, or Coldness, are no more really in them, than Sickness or Pain is in* Manna. Take away the Sensation of them; let not the Eyes see Light, or Colours, nor the Ears hear Sounds; let the Palate not Taste, nor the Nose Smell, and all Colours, Tastes, Odors, and Sounds, as they are such particular *Ideas,* vanish and cease, and are reduced to their Causes, *i.e.* Bulk, figure, and Motion of Parts.[14]

Locke maintains that the secondary qualities are mere dispositions to cause certain sorts of sensations in perceivers. In Locke's account properties such as color are properties of external objects but not on a par with the primary qualities such as shape. Although objects possess primary qualities in themselves, they have their secondary qualities only by virtue of their dispositions to produce sensations in perceivers. As a consequence, if the sensations are removed, the secondary qualities vanish as well.

With Locke, subjectivism about the secondary qualities has reached its mature form; this form of subjectivism with respect to color will be one of the main concerns of this book. The Lockean analysis of the secondary qualities is still one of the more common positions taken by philosophers on this question. The two main features of this sort of view are that there are a limited number of fundamental properties possessed by objects and that properties other than these fundamental ones are to be analyzed in terms of dispositions. In the case of the sensible qualities, the relevant dispositions are ones to produce certain kinds of experiences in perceiving subjects. The essential features of this sort of subjectivism about color will be discussed in more detail later. The list of primary qualities is typically taken from those that occur in the scientific theories of the time. For Locke, this meant that the primary qualities were those of the corpuscalarian philosophy, while for contemporary philosophers it is those properties which are used by physical scientists that are taken to be fundamental. One of the clear signs of a subjectivist analysis of the secondary qualities is the claim that in the absence of perceiving subjects those qualities would not exist.

The discussion so far has focused on the nature of the distinction between primary and secondary qualities in general and not on the nature of color itself. In the works of Newton we find an analysis of color that although clearly compatible with the subjectivism about

[14]Ibid, Bk. II, Chap. VIII, §17.

secondary qualities found in Locke, goes beyond it to offer a more detailed account of the nature of color. Newton offers the following definition in the *Opticks*:

> The homogeneal Light and Rays which appear red, or rather make Objects appear so, I call Rubrifick or Red-making; those which make Objects appear yellow, green, blue, and violet, I call Yellow-making, Green-making, Blue-making, Violet-making, and so of the rest. And if at any time I speak of Light and Rays as coloured or endued with Colours, I would be understood to speak not philosophically and properly, but grossly, and accordingly to such Conceptions as vulgar People in seeing all these Experiments would be apt to frame. For the Rays to speak properly are not coloured. In them there is nothing else than a certain Power and Disposition to stir up a Sensation of this or that Colour . . . so Colours in the Object are nothing but their Dispositions to propagate this or that Motion into the Sensorium, and in the Sensorium they are Sensations of those Motions under the Forms of Colours.[15]

Newton's definition contains the first statement of a conception of color that I call *the wavelength conception of color*. This conception of color has been very influential among both scientists and philosophers.

Although it is anachronistic to attribute to Newton a conception of color that involves wavelengths, all the essential features of the modern form of this view of color are to be found in Newton. The distinguishing characteristic of the wavelength conception is that it takes color to be an illumination-dependent property. This view is implicit in the definition just quoted and Newton explicitly makes this claim in other places in his writing on optics. In his first published paper, the "New theory about light and colors," Newton makes the claim that:

> The Colours of all natural Bodies have no other origin than this, that they are variously qualified to reflect one sort of light in greater plenty than another. And this I have experimented in a dark Room by illuminating those bodies with uncompounded light of divers colours. For by that means any body may be made to appear of any colour. They have there no appropriate colour, but ever appear of the colour of the light cast upon them.[16]

He continues to analyze the colors of the red substance minium and the blue substance bise saying:

[15]Isaac Newton, *Opticks*, NY: Dover Publications, 1979, Bk. I, Part II, Prop II, Theor. II.

[16]Newton, "New theory about light and colors," Prop. 13.

And therefore *Minium* reflecteth Rays of any colour, but most copiously those indued red; and consequently when illustrated with daylight . . . those qualified with red shall abound most in the reflected
light, and by their prevalence cause it to appear of that colour. And
for the same reason *Bise*, reflecting blew most copiously, shall appear
blew by the excess of those Rays in its reflected light; and the like of
other bodies.[17]

He makes similar claims in the *Optica* and in the *Opticks*.[18] In
Newton's view, the kind of light that an object is reflecting determines its color. Since the kind of light an object reflects on a particular occasion is partly determined by the kind of light which illuminates it, its color will vary with changing illumination. For
Newton, color is attributed to objects solely in terms of the light
they reflect.

The analysis of color in terms of properties of light is not the only
component of Newton's definition of color. He analyzes the color of
light in terms of its disposition to cause certain kinds of experiences
in perceivers. This is the basis of his famous claim that "the rays
are not coloured." In his later writings Newton is usually careful to
refer to the various kinds of light as red-making, or blue-making
etc. Combined with his views on the role of light in color
phenomena is a dispositional account of the colors of light rays of
the sort we are already familiar with from Boyle and Locke.
Objects have their color from the kind of light they reflect and
light has its color from its disposition to produce color sensations.
As a result of his discovery of the heterogeneity of white light,
Newton was able to supplement a dispositional account of color
with an account of some of the physics involved. The success of his
new theory of light helped establish the wavelength conception of
color and also helped determine the nature of the research on color
and color vision carried out for the next two hundred years.
Theories of the sort proposed by Newton provide the strongest
opposition for objectivist analyses. In order to defend an objectivist
theory of color successfully it is necessary to defend it against
dispositional analyses and to refute the wavelength conception of
color.

---

[17]Ibid. Bise is a blue or green pigment prepared from smalt, which is
a glass colored blue by cobalt. Minium is a red pigment, either
vermilion or red lead.

[18]Newton, *Optica*, in *The Optical Papers of Isaac Newton: Vol. 1*,
edited by Alan E. Shapiro, Pt. II, Lect. 9, Prop. 5, and *Opticks*, Bk I, Pt. II,
Prop. X.

In the nineteenth century the psychology and physiology of color vision began to be investigated more systematically, and we find the roots there of the peculiar neuro-physiological denial of the objectivity of colors that Zeki espouses in the quote at the beginning of this chapter. This particular analysis of the secondary qualities can be traced to the conclusions drawn by Johannes Müller from his principle of the specific energies of nerves. Müller's principle was an attempt to account for the fact that the same stimulus can produce different sensations depending on the sense organ stimulated. Pressure on the eye produces an experience of light while pressure on the hand results in a sensation of touch. Müller proposed that the different sensations result from the different properties of the nerves stimulated. This principle led him to the conclusion that "The immediate objects of the perception of our senses are merely particular states induced in the nerves."[19] Although some external properties are perceived by means of these nervous states, this is not the case with the secondary qualities. The secondary qualities, including color, taste, and odor, "are to be regarded rather as sensations or modes of reaction of the nerves of sense."[20] Müller's views were very influential and have had an effect on the thinking of psychologists into the present century. Even Helmholtz, although not consistently, makes statements that seem to attribute colors to the brain rather than to external objects or to mental items. In a popular lecture given in 1878, "The Facts in Perception," he makes the claim that the secondary qualities are all properties of the nervous system. He says: "The objects extant in space namely appear to us clothed in the qualities of our sensations. To us they appear red or green, cold or warm, to have a smell or taste, etc., whereas after all these qualities of sensation belong only to our nervous system and do not reach out at all into external space."[21] With Helmholtz we are almost into the twentieth century, and all the main variants of subjectivism with which I will be concerned have been proposed. Our task now is to sort out the essential components of subjectivism with respect to color as a preparation for showing its ultimate untenability.

[19]Müller, *Handbuch der Physiologie des Menschen,* quoted in Herrnstein and Boring, *A Source Book in the History of Psychology,* p. 33.

[20]Ibid., p. 33.

[21]Helmholtz, "The Facts in Perception," in *Hermann von Helmholtz: Epistemological Writings,* edited by Robert S. Cohen and Yehuda Elkana, p. 128.

As we have seen, it has been historically quite important that colors are not to be found among the fundamental properties used by natural scientists to explain the behavior of matter. It was certainly an important consideration for Locke that colors and the other secondary qualities did not figure in the science of his day. Locke is not the only one to have found the scientific uselessness of colors to be compelling evidence that they are not to be treated in the same way as qualities such as shape or electric charge. In his book *Perception*, Jackson argues for the subjectivity of colors by way of the premise, "Either colour is a scientific property or it is not a property of material things."[22] For Jackson, a scientific property is "a property appealed to by current science in explaining the causal effect of one material thing on another material thing, or a logical consequence of such a property or properties."[23] According to Jackson, color does not appear in any currently accepted scientific explanations, and so he concludes that color is not a property of material things. One of the themes running through the history of the primary-secondary quality distinction is the one emphasized by Jackson: only the properties that are needed for current science are the ones that we have reason to attribute to material objects.

It is certainly true that color does not figure in the explanations of contemporary physical scientists. Jackson's argument, as it is stated, does require one obvious caveat: in so far as we are interested in the laws governing the behavior of organisms, color may play an important role. Aside from the question of whether or not psychology should be counted as one of the sciences capable of legitimizing properties, there is another problem with Jackson's argument that does not depend on controversial claims about the stature of psychology. Even given that color does not figure in the explanations of contemporary physical scientists, the possibility still remains open that color is a perfectly objective property of material objects. There are, after all, many objective properties of material objects that do not figure in the explanations of scientists. Given any property or properties that do figure in scientific explanations, we can, using various logical or mathematical techniques, construct indefinitely many other properties from the given ones. For example, given length in centimeters we can construct the property 'having a length which rounded off to the nearest centimeter is odd'. Another constructed property is 'distance from Hoover Tower'. These properties, although all perfectly objective

[22]Jackson, *Perception*, p. 127.
[23]Ibid., p. 122.

and properties of material things will generally not figure in the explanations of scientists. This sort of property may be what Jackson had in mind when he included logical consequences of scientific properties among the scientific properties, although strictly speaking properties do not have logical consequences. In any event, the current practice of scientists is not enough by itself to decide the question of the objectivity of color, even granting the claim that science provides the basis for a complete inventory of the real properties of objects.

There is no contradiction involved in maintaining at the same time the objectivity of color and the absolute unimportance of color in explaining the interactions of material things. Colors could be complex and physically uninteresting constructions out of more fundamental physical properties. It is important not to confuse the explanatory interest of a property with its objectivity. A property can be perfectly objective and still have no important role to play in the scientific explanation of any material phenomena. An example of such a property is the one just constructed. The property of having a length that, rounded off to the nearest centimeter, is odd is unlikely to figure in any scientific explanation of the behavior of material things. Similarly, distance from Hoover tower is not a property found in any of the laws of physics. In spite of their explanatory irrelevance, these properties are clearly objective.

One test for objectivity of a property is the possibility of building a device that can measure the property or determine whether or not a given object possesses the property. If it is possible to build a device that will determine whether or not an object has a given property, then we have established that possession of that property is not dependent on subjective factors. On the basis of this test, the constructed property discussed above is clearly objective. It would be perfectly possible, if not particularly interesting, to construct a device that, given an object, reported whether or not its length in centimeters was odd. It would also be possible, if somewhat more difficult, to construct a device that measured distance from Hoover Tower. I will show later that measurement of color is also possible, and that the characteristics of such measurements reveal interesting facts about the nature of human color vision.

The causal inefficacy of color and the other secondary qualities does not entail that information about the instantiation of these qualities has no interest or practical value. Colors, although not often causes, may be reliable indicators of other properties. For example, edibility of fruits and vegetables is often associated with characteristic changes in their color as anyone who has eaten a green tomato can testify. Colors also play an important role in the identification and re-identification of objects. The colors of objects in general persist over time, and this fact allows us to make use of the color of an object as an aid to visually recognizing it. In fact, without the perception of color we are unable to visually perceive anything at all. It will be clear later that it is no accident that every object we visually perceive is seen as having some color. In any event, the main point is that we can grant Jackson's claim that colors do not figure in any scientific explanation without concluding, as he does, that this fact establishes that colors are not properties of material things. There are many properties that material things have that are very unlikely to occur in the explanations of physical scientists and, for all Jackson has said, color may be among them.

Philosophers sometimes mistakenly assume that the lack of scientific usefulness of a property implies the subjectivity of that property. Another confusion of this sort to be guarded against is confusing anthropocentrism with subjectivity. Scientists are interested in explaining phenomena using properties and concepts that are, as far as is possible, independent of peculiar human limitations and characteristics. Scientific explanations attempt to abstract away from the particular perceptual perspective from which human beings view the world. Properties that are connected with characteristics of the human perceptual system, such as apparent size, play no role in the physical sciences. It may be possible to explain why one object looks bigger than another, but the fact that one object appears to be bigger than another cannot figure in any explanation of the behavior of the objects. As we have seen, however, failure to be useful to physical scientists is no mark of the subjective. Similarly, some kinds of human-centeredness are compatible with objectivity.

This compatibility has sometimes been denied by philosophers. J. J. C. Smart once argued that colors cannot be objective on the basis of their supposed anthropocentrism. According to Smart:

> The colours seen by a normal percipient do not depend on any simple property of the object seen, but . . . depend partly on the special peculiarities of the human visual apparatus. This makes very unplausible the Objectivist view that what we see in colour vision corresponds to some intrinsic *quale* of the external object. If the *quale* had been correlated with something simple like a wavelength of emitted or reflected monochromatic light the Objectivist theory would have been a little more plausible. We have seen, however, that the *quale* would have to be correlated with something much more complicated which depends idiosyncratically on the characteristics of the human eye and

nervous system. That this should be so is quite as unbelievable as astrology.[24]

This argument makes the mistake of confusing arbitrariness with subjectivity. The mistake made by astrologers is not in supposing that the heavens can be divided into various constellations. Dividing the heavens in this way is a more or less arbitrary task, but once it has been done the divisions are perfectly objective. The mistake in astrology is to suppose that these divisions are meaningful in terms of their causal relations to human fortune. The problem with astrology is a belief in bizarre causal laws, not an arbitrary structure imposed upon the stars.

Although the division of the heavens into constellations is arbitrary, it is nevertheless useful to astronomers. Astronomy requires some method of referring to the locations of stars in the celestial sphere, and the use of constellations fulfills at least part of this function. Although more precise systems exist, the use of constellations for locating stars allows one to find a star in the heavens without instruments and without having to visually estimate such quantities as right ascension. This brings up the more general point that systems of classification that are quite arbitrary in terms of the underlying structure of the classified entities can nevertheless be quite useful. Anthropocentrism is just a special form of arbitrariness, and anthropocentric classifications can often be useful in the same way as any other arbitrary but objective way of classifying objects.

It is an undeniable fact that the way the world appears to us is the joint product of the way the world is and the way we are. Perception is a highly idiosyncratic process and the nature of the information about the external world that we are given in perception is strongly dependent on the characteristics and limitations of our perceptual systems. Our language is equally infected with our point of view. We should not be surprised, then, if the description in physical terms of what two objects must have in common in order for them to appear to have the same color looks

---

[24]J.J.C. Smart, "Colours," *Philosophy* 36 (1961), p. 132. Smart is using the term *quale* in a sense somewhat different from its modern use to refer to phenomenal characteristics of experience. There is an older use in which a *quale* is any property considered as an independent existent. It is only fair to Smart to point out that he later changed his mind on this issue and came to hold a view similar in many respects to the one I will defend. See Smart, "On some criticisms of a physicalist theory of colors," in *Philosophical Aspects of the Mind–Body Problem*, edited by Chung–ying Cheng.

highly arbitrary. From the point of view of physics, the color discriminations made by human perceivers are highly arbitrary. Similarly, the extension of our common color terms such as "red" are also very bizarre when considered physically. Physics, however, does not provide a complete catalog of those properties that are objective. As long as the properties corresponding to our color language and our color perceptions can be analyzed in terms of the scientific vocabulary given us by the physical sciences, the objectivity of color language and perception will be sustainable. What will be true is that the specification in physical terms of those aspects of color that we see and talk about will depend on prior knowledge of the characteristics of the human visual system.

One of the common claims made about secondary qualities in our historical survey is that in the absence of perceiving subjects, the secondary qualities would vanish from the world leaving objects with only their primary qualities. As we have seen, this claim has been made Galileo, Boyle and Locke. The absence of secondary qualities from a world without perceivers follows from the relational analysis, given the secondary qualities in such accounts. The redness of an object, according to Locke, consists in its disposition to produce sensations of red in human perceivers. If there are no human perceivers, it seems that there could be no grounds for attributing such a disposition to objects. Given the apparent intimate connection between colors and perceivers, this conclusion has a certain intuitive plausibility. We have already acknowledged the unimportance of color in the causal interactions of material things and the unnaturalness of color from the point of view of physics. Colors seem to take their being from the existence of those subjects that perceive them. In denying reality to colors in a world that lacked perceivers, Locke seems to be on firm ground.

There is another alternative, however, that accounts for the same intuitions that give the subjectivist account its plausibility. We can admit that the kinds of colors that human beings see and talk about are only of interest because of their connection with human perceivers. The colors we see, although their interest and their specification in physical terms derive from the existence of human perceivers, do not depend for their existence on the existence of human perceivers. In a world in which there were no human beings, these kinds of colors would continue to exist, although they would be of absolutely no interest. Our intuitions that talk of color in a world without perceiving creatures would somehow be misguided derives from the absolute uninformativeness of such talk in such a world. There would be color, but since color plays little role in the causal laws that govern a world without perceivers, it would tell us little of interest in such a world.

The two characteristics of color, causal irrelevance and anthropocentrism, are characteristics that are often assumed to be marks of the lack of objectivity of a property. The objectivity of color can be defended, however, without claiming that colors have any important role in the causal structure of the world or that the information about objects conveyed in color talk and perception is anything but anthropocentric. These traditional accompaniments of subjectivism are perfectly compatible with the form of objectivism defended here. This slightly attenuated variety of realism can be called *anthropocentric realism*. Anthropocentric realism has the virtue of not claiming more for our knowledge of the external world than can be realistically expected, given the limited sort of creatures that we are. An anthropocentric realist can acknowledge the partial nature of the information about physical objects that is available in perception and at the same time defend the objectivity of this information. The anthropocentric realist not only admits but makes a point of the fact that the sort of knowledge we are able to obtain perceptually depends on the peculiar characteristics of our perceptual apparatus. The categories of perceptual knowledge may differ from those that are scientifically useful without impairing the objectivity of those categories. In fact, as we will see in the case of color, the categories of common sense knowledge are often reducible to the categories of physical science. It is this emphasis on the objectivity of these categories that makes the anthropocentric realist a realist. Anthropocentric realism about color is a form of reductive realism. Colors are identical with a certain complex and derivative physical property of the surfaces of objects. This property is both causally irrelevant and anthropocentric in nature. Nevertheless, it is possible to specify the property 'red', for example, in terms that make no reference to human nature or human experience. It is this fact, the specification without reference to features of human experience, that is essential to objectivity. If it can be shown that objects have their colors independently of the subjective experiences of human perceivers, then the objectivity of color will have been established.

It is important to emphasize this last point: that a property is objective if and only if its possession by an object is independent of the nature or even existence of experiences of that property. A view such as Locke's comes out as subjective on this criterion since whether or not an object has a given color depends on the subjective nature of the experiences it is disposed to produce. It is perfectly compatible with Locke's view that there is an independently specifiable property or objective ground that underlies the disposition to produce color experiences. That is to say that given the current laws of physics and characteristics of the human perceptual system this objective ground may be a reliable indicator of the presence of the relevant disposition. An anthropocentric realist and a Lockean subjectivist can agree on all the relevant empirical facts. The disagreement comes in whether color is identified with the disposition of objects to produce the relevant experiences or with the objective ground of that disposition. The only fact relevant to objectivity is whether color has its existence and character independently of the existence and character of perceiving subjects. Although it is possible to eliminate some philosophical accounts of color on empirical grounds, the question of the objectivity of color is in the end a conceptual one. To settle the question, we need to discover which way of conceptualizing color allows us to account for both pre-theoretic intuitions regarding color and the wide range of known color phenomena.

In arguing for the objectivity of color, we can make use of experiments and theories from the psychology of color vision. This empirical work is relevant to the philosophical enterprise in two different ways. First, some philosophical arguments and analyses of color assume that color perception has certain characteristics. For example, the wavelength conception of color derived from Newton has had an impact on the thinking of philosophers about color. The illumination dependence of color that follows from this conception is thought to be supported by the variability of perceived color with lighting conditions. The experimental literature on the variation of perceived color with lighting conditions shows, however, that perceived color is in many circumstances constant through changes in illumination. This phenomenon is known as color constancy. Chapter 4 discusses how experiments demonstrating color constancy done by Edwin Land cast doubt on the wavelength conception of light. As a result, an important philosophical conception of the nature of color is seen to be associated with a false view of the nature of color perception. Attention to work done in psychology is necessary to make sure that philosophical theories do not derive their support from presuppositions or have implications that conflict with the empirical data.

The second way in which work in psychology is relevant, especially to physicalist analyses of color, is to provide evidence that it is actually possible to obtain information perceptually about the proposed candidate for color. I will argue that color is identical with the characteristic ways objects have of reflecting light. I will make this proposal more precise in later chapters. The point here is that it could turn out that it is not possible for our perceptions of color to be correlated appropriately with the proposed candidate for color. If it is impossible for the visual system to determine whether or not an object has the proposed property, then color, in such an analysis, would turn out to be epistemologically inaccessible. There would be very little point to defending an objectivist view of color that has as a consequence that we are never able to see the colors of things. Land's theoretical explanation of his experimental results gets part of the way towards showing that my analysis of color is not subject to this sort of objection. A more recent theory proposed by Laurence Maloney and Brian Wandell provides even more striking support for the anthropocentric realist analysis of color. The work of Maloney and Wandell shows that by assuming that the function of color vision is the determination of the reflecting properties of objects, it is possible to develop a powerful and coherent theory of color vision. Their work provides the demonstration of perceptual possibility that the anthropocentric realist theory requires.

In spite of these ways in which empirical science is relevant to the philosophical issues, it is nevertheless, a mistake to think that all the philosophical issues surrounding color can be settled by appeal to psychological theories. There are still real philosophical issues, both metaphysical and conceptual, regarding the nature of color that must be settled. Psychologists themselves disagree on the implications of their research for some of these issues. For example, Land, whose work I cite in arguing for objectivism, is himself a species of subjectivist. Land believes that colors are the creation of the brain mechanisms that compute color descriptions based on retinal stimuli. According to Land, "What we know as reality is the experience at the terminal end of this computation. Since we all use the same computation mechanism, we share the terminal experiences. We name them, talk about them, train ourselves to relate to them and to handle them."[25] Although Land's view is misguided, this point is not settled by his empirical work one way or the other. Other workers in the field come to the opposite conclusion on the basis of similar facts. Maloney claims that

[25]Land, "Recent advances in retinex theory and some implications for cortical computations: Color vision and the natural image," *Proc. Natl. Acad. Sci. USA* 80 (1983), p. 5164.

his work suggests that color is an objective property.[26] Although it is necessary to have the relevant empirical facts right, such knowledge is not sufficient to settle the important philosophical disputes regarding the nature of color.

It may seem that one of the most important features of the primary-secondary quality distinction as drawn by Locke and his successors has yet to be discussed, namely, Locke's contention "That the *Ideas of primary Qualities* of Bodies, *are Resemblances* of them . . . but the *Ideas, produced* in us *by* these *Secondary Qualities, have no resemblance* of them at all."[27] Mackie defends a similar view when he argues that on the one hand, "A large part of the basis of a thing's power to produce the idea of squareness will . . . be its literally being square, its having a shape-quality which is just like the shape-quality which we find in the experiential content to which the thing gives rise";[28] while on the other, "Colours as we see them are totally different not only from the powers to produce such sensations . . . but also from the ground or basis of these powers in the things that we call coloured."[29] In other words, there is nothing in objects like color as we see it although objects do have shapes as we see them. This is Locke's famous doctrine of the lack of resemblance between the ideas of the secondary qualities and their correlates in objects.

It is difficult to know what to make of Locke's claim that our idea of shape resembles shape as it is in objects, while our idea of color has no resemblance to anything in the object. If we interpret Locke as claiming that there is resemblance between our experiences of shape, considered as experiences, and shape, then the thesis is absurd. George Berkeley was certainly saying *something* true when he claimed that "an idea can be like nothing but an idea."[30] What it is like for me to see a square does not in the least resemble a square. Experiences have no spatial properties, let alone the particular ones that may be assigned to their content. In this interpretation of the resemblance thesis, the problem is not with the claim that ideas of color do not resemble any quality in objects but with the claim that ideas of primary qualities *do* resemble qualities of objects. There is no sense to be made of the claim that

[26]Laurence Maloney, *Computational Approaches to Color Constancy,* Doctoral dissertation, Stanford University, 1984, p. 119.

[27]Locke, *Essay*, Bk. II, Chap. VIII, § 15.

[28]Mackie, *Problems From Locke*, Oxford: Clarendon Press, 1976, p. 15.

[29]Ibid., p. 14.

[30]George Berkeley, *A Treatise Concerning the Principles of Human Knowledge*, Indianapolis: Hackett, 1982, Part I, § 8.

an experience of squareness resembles physical squareness. Even if we assume some sort of materialist reduction of experiences to brain states, there is no reason to believe that visual experiences of squareness will be instantiated in square regions of the brain. This reading of the resemblance thesis is completely indefensible.

The interpretation just considered is not, however, the only way to understand Locke's claim about the difference between primary and secondary qualities. According to Jonathan Bennett, the only plausible way to understand the resemblance thesis is to see it as claiming that "in causally explaining ideas of primary qualities, one uses the same words in describing the causes as in describing the effects (shape-ideas, etc., are caused by shapes etc.); whereas in causally explaining ideas of secondary qualities one must describe the causes in one vocabulary and the effects in another (colour-ideas, etc., are caused by shapes, etc.)."[31] Whether or not Bennett's interpretation represents Locke's own view will not concern us here. I will only argue that the resemblance thesis as interpreted by Bennett poses no obstacle to defending the objectivity of colors. Taken one way, Bennett's reading of the resemblance thesis is merely a special case of the causal irrelevance of color, a claim that does not conflict with the objectivity of color. Colors are no more effective in physiology than they are in physics. Of course, shape and the other traditional primary qualities are also of little interest for sensory physiology. The fact that color may not play any role in an explanation of color perception does not establish that colors are not objective. Bennett's interpretation of the resemblance thesis is irrelevant to the objectivity of color.

There is a sense, however, in which color plays the same role in explanations of the perception of color that shape plays in the explanation of shape perception. I will argue that color is to be identified with the disposition objects have to reflect varying percentages of the ambient light. Since this disposition affects the characteristics of the light reaching the eye, which is the stimulus for color perception, it plays a crucial role in the causal chain responsible for color perception. Similarly, the shape of an object affects the way in which it reflects light and consequently the shape of an object plays the same sort of role as does its other reflecting properties. In addition to the relative importance of shape as opposed to color in explaining the causal interactions of objects, there is another difference relevant to the points just made.

[31]Jonathan Bennett, *Locke, Berkeley, Hume: Central Themes*, Oxford: Clarendon Press, 1971, p. 106.

Any exercise of the disposition an object has to reflect fixed proportions of the light illuminating it will always be capable of explanation in more fundamental terms. We can always explain the reflecting powers of objects in more fundamental physical terms. The causal effects of shapes will not be capable of more fundamental explanations in this way. But again, the fact that a property is derivative is no threat to its objectivity.

The last interpretation of the resemblance thesis that I will consider is less obviously flawed than the first two and is also arguably more consistent with what Locke actually says on the subject. Mackie offers and defends an interpretation of the resemblance thesis that makes use of the notion of the intentional object of an idea or perception. According to Mackie, our perceptual experiences come with specific content: they present the world to us as being a particular way. When I see that an object is square, I have an experience that has as its content a square object. The intentional object of my perception is distinct from the physical object that is the cause of my perception. I can see an object as square without its actually being square. An object being represented to me as being square is distinct from the squareness of that object. Another way of expressing this idea is in terms of how things look. According to Mackie, "To say that there is an intentional object of a certain sort is only to say . . . that that is how things look (or feel or sound, and so on) to the person in question."[32] In this interpretation of Locke, ideas in the sense of the resemblance thesis are intentional objects. They are the contents of perceptions, and not the perceptions themselves.

Given this interpretation of Locke's use of 'idea', we can make sense of the resemblance thesis in a way that avoids the objections to the two preceding readings of that thesis. According to Mackie:

> To say that an objective quality resembles the idea of that quality is simply to say that in this respect things are just as they look in a strictly sensory sense of 'look' . . . to say that there is nothing in the things like an idea of a certain class is to say that things are not at all as they sensorily appear in this respect.[33]

That is to say, ideas of shape resemble shapes in that our perceptions of shape represent things to us just as they are. By making resemblance depend on the contents of sensory experiences rather than the characters of the experiences *qua* experiences, Mackie avoids the Berkeleyan criticism of the first interpretation of the

[32]Mackie, *Problems From Locke*, p. 48.
[33]Ibid., pp. 49–50.

resemblance thesis. Since Mackie's thesis does not depend on the causal irrelevance of the secondary qualities for its content, it avoids the charge of confusing causal efficacy with objectivity that Bennett's interpretation succumbed to. There is something compelling in Mackie's idea that our perceptual experiences represent the world to us as being a certain way, but even granting this the resemblance thesis cannot be defended.

In this interpretation of the resemblance thesis, we are to understand Locke as claiming that there is no property in objects that corresponds to colors as we see them. Our perceptions of color represent the world to us as being a way that it is not. In so far as our perceptions lead us to take objects to be literally colored in the way we see colors. our perceptions are misleading. Science tells us that there are properties corresponding to our ideas of shape and the other primary qualities, but if there is any ground in objects for our perceptions of color, this ground is a certain complex of primary qualities. The intentional objects of our color experiences are not complexes of primary qualities and consequently our perceptions of color are misleading in this respect, or so the argument runs. There are problems with the analysis of perceptual content that underlies this form of the resemblance thesis but they are not of concern here. Even on its own terms, Mackie's apparatus cannot support the ontological distinction it is being used to make. It is perfectly consistent with the intentional object interpretation of the resemblance thesis and the findings of modern science that there are colors as we see them.

Mackie's (and supposedly Locke's) claim depends on the content of our color experiences excluding the possibility that colors are complexes of primary qualities. If it is compatible with the content of our perceptions of color that color is a derivative physical property, then the distinction between primary and secondary qualities is blurred. Science only tells us that there is no reason to believe that objects have colors over and above all the properties that occur in the explanations of physical scientists. There is no incompatibility with science if color turns out to be possession of a particular complex of primary qualities. Colors as we see them may not make the primary quality ground of color obvious, but all that is necessary is that there be no conflict between the content of our color experiences and their analysis in terms of primary qualities.

Color as we see it is notorious for defying analysis in terms of other concepts. Our experiences of color are simple in the sense that they provide no clue about the connection of color with any other property. This has sometimes been taken to establish that the content of our color experiences is unanalyzable. There is another possibility, however, and that is that our experiences of color are essentially lacking in content. This view of the content of color concepts is proposed by D.M. Armstrong. He asks:

> Suppose that our concept of red is *all* blank or gap? May it not be that we know *nothing* about what redness is in its own nature? May it not be that we only know contingent truths about redness—such truths as that it is a property detected by the eye and possessed, or apparently possessed, by such things as the surface of ripe tomatoes and Jonathan apples?[34]

Our perceptions of color represent the world as being a certain way but do not place any substantive constraints on what that way is. In Armstrong's view, a perception that an object is red tells us that that object is similar in certain respects to other red things but tells us nothing about what respects those may be.

Armstrong's argument for the emptiness of color concepts is consistent with the emphasis on partial information that is an important part of anthropocentric realism. Color perception delivers information about the variations in a particular derivative physical property but does not specify what that property might be. The resemblance thesis will pose no objection to the identification of color with this physical property since our ideas of color are so largely vacuous. Armstrong goes too far, however, in maintaining the emptiness of our concept of color. Color is not a completely simple concept and the various colors stand in certain complex relationships to each other. It is something like a necessary truth that yellow is brighter than brown or that pink is more similar to red than it is to blue. I will show that these internal relations among colors can be accounted for in a reductive account of colors. Nevertheless, it will be my assumption that our perceptions of color tell us very little about what color is in objects; my main defense of this assumption will be the success of the following account.

There are two general sorts of problems that must be faced by any attempt to defend an objectivist analysis of color. One contention of subjectivists about color has been that our color experiences are incoherent. The claim is that there is no way to consistently attribute colors to objects since our experiences of color attribute conflicting colors to one and the same object. The other problem is raised by the claim that there is conflict between the conceptual

---

[34]D.M. Armstrong, *A Materialist Theory of the Mind*, NY: Humanities Press, 1968, p. 275.

scheme of science and that part of common sense that attributes color to objects. Both these attacks on the objectivity of color attempt to show that it is incoherent to attribute colors to objects on the basis of our perception of color. They attempt to show that colors cannot be objective by showing not merely that there is in fact no objective analysis of color but that there cannot be such an analysis.

In Chapter 2, I discuss an argument of the first type. In *the argument from microscopes*, Berkeley attempted to establish that there is a conflict between perception of color with the naked eye and perception of color through a microscope. Berkeley's example is a drop of blood which appears uniformly red to the naked eye but appears to be composed of red corpuscles in a clear fluid when viewed through a microscope. Berkeley argues that one and the same drop of blood cannot be both red all over and red and clear and that consequently we must suppose that one or both of the perceptions of the color of the drop of blood is illusory. This argument, if successful, would pose a serious challenge to an objectivist theory of colors. It would seem that since the microscope gives us more detailed information about the colors of objects, the appearance presented through the microscope is the one to be identified as the true color of the drop. This position is one that Armstrong endorses. To take this position, however, leaves the objectivist in the somewhat awkward position of defending the objectivity of colors while claiming that we have very limited perceptual access to these objective colors.

I show that Berkeley's argument is unsound. One reconstruction of the argument depends on a premise to the effect that it is one and the same object that appears red to the naked eye and red and clear through the microscope. This premise is needed in order to apply *the exclusion principle*, which states that one and the same object cannot be more than one color (or set of colors) all over. In Berkeley's example, however, it is not one and the same object that presents these different appearances but rather an object and some of its parts. If we revise the argument to take this into account we need to replace the exclusion principle with *the dissectivity principle*. This principle states that the parts of a colored thing must be both colored all over and the same color as the thing itself. I then argue that there is no reason to believe the dissectivity principle. At heart, Berkeley's argument depends on a failure to take seriously the partial nature of perception. When we look at a thing and fail to see the color of its parts or that it has any parts, we are not seeing that it does not have any parts. We are unable to determine perceptually all aspects of an object's color from any given perspective; once this is realized the argument from microscopes loses its persuasiveness.

I also consider an argument for subjectivism of the second type that is flawed in ways similar to the argument from microscopes. Bruce Aune has argued that the conceptual scheme of science leaves no space for colors as we commonly conceive them. His argument depends on a modified form of the dissectivity principle and consequently fails for the same reason as the argument from microscopes.

The two arguments just discussed attempt to show that objectivism about colors is incoherent or in conflict with the conceptual scheme of science. Other philosophers have attempted to argue that although it is possible that color might be identified with some physical property there is no such property. Chapters 3 and 4 consider one such argument of Keith Campbell's but, more importantly, in the course of exposing problems with Campbell's argument, also show that some common philosophical assumptions about the nature of color and color perception are false. These assumptions are what constitute the wavelength conception of color. The distinctive feature of this conception of color is that it limits the possible candidates for the nature of color in objects to properties of light. This limitation is found at the beginnings of modern views on the physical nature of color and was first put forward by Newton. In this conception, color, if it is anything in objects at all, is the power that an object has to reflect light of a given character. The wavelength conception has one immediate and important consequence: since the character of the light reflected by an object is the joint product of the nature of the object's surface and the character of the illumination, colors are illumination dependent. In this conception of color, objects will change their color with every change in the illumination. If we take this point of view, then we must deny one of the most important features of our common sense conception of color: the stability and illumination independence of color.

Campbell also uses this conception to argue that there is no suitable physical property with which to identify color. He shows that there is little correlation between perceived color and any characteristic of the light an object is reflecting at a given time. Since one requirement for the identification of two properties is that they be coextensive, Campbell's argument seems to have accomplished its task. If we must search for the objective basis of color among the characteristics of light, then the search has

failed. There is no characteristic of light suitable for identification with color.

The conception of color which Campbell is using, however, is
fundamentally mistaken. To suppose that color must be correlated
with properties of light is a mistake, although a popular mistake.
A well-known fact about human color vision shows that this conception of color is mistaken. Human color vision displays what is
known as color constancy. Color constancy is the familiar phenomenon that the apparent colors of objects are relatively independent of the character of the illumination under which they are
viewed. Although the spectral composition of daylight changes
markedly throughout the day and with the weather, the apparent
colors of objects change little, if it all, with time of day or degree of
cloudiness. This sort of constancy exists even when viewing abstract
shapes and there are no cues as to the nature of the illumination.
The existence of color constancy establishes the lack of correlation
between perceived color and any characteristic of light but at the
same time suggests another possibility for the objective basis of
color. This property is surface spectral reflectance.

The surface spectral reflectance of an object is its disposition to
reflect different amounts of light at different wavelengths. A given
object will, in general, reflect a fixed percentage of the light
illuminating it at every wavelength.[35] It is possible to measure
surface spectral reflectance by taking the ratio between the incident
and reflected light at each wavelength in the visible spectrum. In
conjunction with the spectral power distribution (the distribution of
power in light with respect to wavelength) of the illumination the
reflectance of an object determines the character of the light
reflected by an object. As a matter of empirical fact in many situations outside the psychological laboratory, perceived color is much
more closely correlated with the surface spectral reflectance of the
object being viewed than it is with the spectral power distribution
of the light reaching the eye from that surface.

This fact suggests the principal thesis of this work: color is surface spectral reflectance. If this identification can be successfully
defended, then the objectivity of colors will be established. Colors

[35]There are surfaces whose reflectance changes with exposure to light.
Photographic film is one common example of a surface of this type.
Some common paint pigments also undergo reversible changes in their
reflectance when exposed to light of varying intensities. In my view
these changes are real changes in color unlike the changes in the
character of the light an object reflects in different illuminations.

are nothing more than the characteristic ways objects have of reflecting light. The surface spectral reflectance of an object is a property that object has completely independently of the existence or nature of perceiving creatures. As such it meets the criteria for objectivity set down earlier. If color is reflectance, then it is possible in principle to determine the colors of objects without making use of the characteristics of human color experience.

Chapter 5 considers an objection to this identification of color with reflectance based on the fact that objects with very different reflectances can, even in normal circumstances, appear to have the same color. Objects with this property are known as metamers. This phenomena is due to fundamental limitations in the ability of the human perceptual system to analyze light according to wavelength. In my account of color, sameness of perceived color is not a perfectly reliable guide to sameness of color. In light of these facts, the identification of color with surface spectral reflectance seems somewhat arbitrary. It seems a highly undesirable consequence of this analysis that there are differences of color undetectable in normal circumstances by human perceivers. There does not seem to be any reason to call such differences, differences in *color*. A dispositional analysis of color, such as Locke's, seems to give a more reasonable account of metamers. In a dispositional view, sameness of perceived color in normal circumstances implies sameness of color.

I argue, however, that the identification of colors with reflectances allows a more satisfactory solution to the problems posed by metamers than does a dispositional view. The key fact that underlies this argument is that any pair of metameric objects will display their difference in reflectance under some illumination. If we choose the right sort of illumination, a pair of objects that appear identical in color under normal circumstances will appear to differ in color. In the anthropocentric realist account of color this perception of color difference will be a veridical perception. In a dispositional analysis, however, such a perception of color difference will be illusory. This puts the dispositionalist in the odd position of supposing that we can see a real physical difference between objects, i.e. a difference in reflectance, by suffering from an illusion of color difference. This fact, that all differences in reflectance will be perceived as color differences under some illuminations, provides a substantial if not conclusive argument for individuating colors in the fine-grained manner required by my account.

Meeting the objections of the dispositionalist to the identification of colors with reflectances does not solve all the problems facing an objectivist account of colors. An account is still needed of the relation between color perception and color language and the reflectances which are colors on this analysis. Sketching the outlines of such an account is the function of Chapter 6. As the dispositionalist emphasizes, not every difference in reflectance corresponds to a difference in perceived color in normal circumstances. The fundamental insight that is needed to provide such an account is that color perception and language give us anthropocentrically defined kinds of colors and not colors themselves. It is this insight that makes it appropriate to describe the sort of realism that I defend as anthropocentric realism. Perception does not reveal the whole truth about colors and the truth it does reveal is delimited by the characteristics of our perceptual systems. Human perception of all properties, not just colors, is indeterminate in the sense that it only delivers partial information about the fully determinate qualities that objects possess. I show that it is possible to characterize the kinds of colors that perception reveals in objective terms. I also argue that the kind of indeterminacy involved in color perception does not differ in any important respect from the sort of indeterminacy involved in primary quality perception. The tools used to classify the indeterminacy involved in perception are also used to sketch the beginnings of an account of English color terms. The basic technique involves recognizing the importance of the characteristics of the human visual system in determining the kinds given in color perception and color language. The nature of our experience only influences which of the many possible kinds of color our color terms and perceptions refer to. The kinds themselves exist independently of our color experience and are fully objective. One way of describing anthropocentric realism with respect to color is that the colors we perceive and talk about are objective although scientifically uninteresting kinds.

With the treatment of color perception and language, all the major obstacles facing an objectivist analysis of color have been dealt with. Identifying color with surface spectral reflectance provides for a coherent account of all the major phenomena of color perception and language. My defense of the objectivity of color is relative , in the sense that I take my task to be showing that there are no problems facing the objectivity of colors that are not equally problems for the objectivity of primary qualities such as shape. If there are problems in giving an adequate account of our perceptual knowledge of shapes they will also be problems for the perception of color and vice versa. The primary focus here is on the ontological status of color, and color perception is discussed only in so far as it is relevant to that issue.

2

THE ARGUMENT FROM MICROSCOPES

I FIRST CONSIDER *the argument from microscopes.*[1] Its classic statement is in Berkeley's *Three Dialogues.*[2] There, it figures as one of several arguments against the reality of colors and the other secondary qualities. These arguments are typically referred to as the arguments from perceptual relativity. Berkeley mentions these arguments in *The Principles* [3] but in that work does not appear to lay much stress on them. The role these arguments play in Berkeley's thought and their importance have been a subject of some debate in the literature on Berkeley. I will not address myself to this issue except in so far as it is relevant to clarifying the structure and presuppositions of this particular argument. The focus here is the argument from microscopes as an obstacle to maintaining the objectivity of colors and not the role it plays in Berkeley's system.

Berkeley is attempting to argue that it is not true that "the colors which we see exist in external bodies." He has already had Hylas concede that some colors are merely apparent and not actually possessed by the object that appears to have them. He follows this concession with his statement of the argument from microscopes.

[1] The name for this argument is taken from Armstrong, "Colour Realism and the Argument from Microscopes," in *The Nature of Mind and Other Essays,* pp 104–118.

[2] A somewhat less clearly defined form of the argument is found in Locke. I will not discuss Locke's version of the argument here. See *Essay* II, XXIII, 11.

[3] Berkeley, *Principles* , secs. 11–15.

PHILONOUS: 'Apparent' colors you call them? How shall we distinguish these apparent colors from real?

HYLAS: Very easily. Those are to be thought apparent which appearing only at a distance, vanish upon a nearer approach.

PHILONOUS: And those, I suppose, are to be thought real which are discovered by the most near and exact survey.

HYLAS: Right.

PHILONOUS: Is the nearest and exactest survey made by the help of a microscope or by the naked eye?

HYLAS: By a microscope, doubtless.

PHILONOUS: But a microscope often discovers colors in an object different from those perceived by the unassisted sight. And, in case we had microscopes magnifying to any assigned degree, it is certain that no object whatsoever, viewed through them, would appear in the same color which it exhibits to the naked eye.

HYLAS: And what will you conclude from all this? You cannot argue that there are really and naturally no colors on objects because by artificial managements they may be altered or made to vanish.

PHILONOUS: I think it may evidently be concluded from your own concessions that all the colors we see with our naked eyes are only apparent as those on the clouds, since they vanish upon a more close and accurate inspection which is afforded us by a microscope.[4]

The conclusion of the argument is that only the colors seen through a microscope have any reality. Berkeley follows this statement of the argument with a discussion of the possibility of organisms with visual systems that differ from those of human beings and then draws the somewhat stronger conclusion: "From all which, should it not seem to follow, that all colors are equally apparent, and that none of those which we perceive are really inherent in any outward object."[5] The conclusion of the argument from microscopes itself is the weaker statement, "That either the appearance of objects to the naked eye or their appearance through the microscope is illusory." For Berkeley, however, this weaker conclusion is only a step towards showing that all colors are equally apparent.

[4]Berkeley, *Three Dialogues between Hylas and Philonous*, Indianapolis: Hackett, 1979, p. 20.
[5]Ibid., p. 21.

Slightly adapted, the argument from microscopes can be applied to other visually perceived properties. Bertrand Russell gives a very similar argument with respect to the visual perception of texture in *The Problems of Philosophy*. He is discussing the visual aspects of a table and has just argued that the table itself does not have any one particular color. He goes on to argue:

> The same thing applies to the texture. With the naked eye one can see the grain, but otherwise the table looks smooth and even. If we looked at it through a microscope, we should see roughnesses and hills and valleys, and all sorts of differences that are imperceptible to the naked eye. Which of these is the 'real' table? We are naturally tempted to say that what we see through the microscope is more real, but that in turn would be changed by a still more powerful microscope. If, then, we cannot trust what we see with the naked eye, why should we trust what we see through a microscope? Thus, again, the confidence in our senses with which we began deserts us.[6]

According to Russell the argument from microscopes applies to the perception of roughness and smoothness as well as to the perception of color.

The argument regarding texture and the argument regarding color share the same form. They both attempt to establish a conflict between perceptions of an object obtained in different circumstances. Both the apparent color of an object and its apparent texture can change as the distance of the object from the perceiver is varied. It is an essential part of the argument to assume that the object cannot consistently have both the properties it appears to have from a distance and the properties it appears to have from closer up. This assumption generates a conflict of appearances. For both texture and color, the argument purports to establish that at least some of our perceptions of those properties must be mistaken. Both Russell and Berkeley then carry the argument one step further and claim that any choice of viewing conditions is arbitrary. The end result is that colors and textures are denied any status as objective properties of external things. This last step is not a necessary part of the argument, however, and it is possible, as Armstrong does, to take the argument as establishing that only the colors seen through a suitable microscope are real.

It is important to note that the facts appealed to in these arguments are familiar to all of us. When I start walking towards the hills behind Stanford they appear a uniform golden color. As I get closer I am able to see more and more detail in the scenery and as a

[6]Bertrand Russell, *The Problems of Philosophy*, Oxford: Oxford University Press, 1975, p. 10.

result see that the hills are covered with plants that are of a variety of different colors. Anyone who has ever looked closely at the screen of a television set has made a discovery of the sort that Russell and Berkeley draw our attention to. The familiarity of these sorts of cases does not, however, lead us to draw the conclusion that Russell and Berkeley would have us draw. We do not find the fact that objects change in their appearance as we move closer to them puzzling nor do we typically infer from this fact that the appearance an object presents from a distance is illusory.

The argument offered by Berkeley attempts to establish that our failure to be puzzled by these cases is mistaken. The conclusion of these arguments entails that many of our color perceptions must be mistaken. If the argument is successful we must either admit that the colors we perceive with the naked eye are often illusory or that instruments such as microscopes do not reveal to us information about the colors of objects viewed using them. Neither horn of the dilemma is compatible with common sense and, in the case of Berkeley, the argument is a step in a complete denial of the objectivity of colors. These arguments are not, however, capable of establishing their intended conclusion although they do demonstrate an important fact about visual perception. In order to see where the flaw in the argument from microscopes lies, it will be helpful to attempt to identify its premises. I will only attempt here to reconstruct the argument as it applies to colors although it should be clear how similar considerations could be applied to visually perceived texture.

The classic example to which the argument from microscopes is applied is that of a drop of blood. A drop of blood which appears uniformly red when viewed with the naked eye will appear to consist of red particles suspended in a clear fluid when viewed through a suitable microscope. The first premise of the argument is simply a description of the phenomena that give the argument its name.

P_1 The drop of blood appears red all over to the naked eye and red and transparent all over when viewed under the microscope.

There are three more premises that are needed in to order to make the argument valid.[7]

[7]This statement of the argument is adapted from Konrad Marc-Wogau, "The Argument from Illusion and Berkeley's Idealism," in *Locke and Berkeley*, edited by C. B. Martin and D. M. Armstrong, pp. 340–352.

P₂ One and the same thing cannot both have one color (or set of colors) and at the same time have a different color (or set of colors) all over. (*The exclusion principle*)

P₃ Being red all over is different from being red and transparent all over in the sense of the exclusion principle.

P₄ The drop of blood which appears red to the naked eye and red and transparent through the microscope is (identically) one and the same object.

These four premises force the conclusion that:

C At least one of the color appearances in P₁ is illusory.

So stated, the argument is valid but not sound, and no plausible variations on it can be made sound.

Before discussing problems with the argument from microscopes, it is important to clarify what conclusions about color it purports to establish and in what way it poses a threat to the objectivity of color. The argument from microscopes itself only establishes the weak conclusion that at least some of our color perceptions are mistaken. In order to establish the conclusion that colors are subjective, it would need to be shown that any choice of viewing conditions under which the true colors of things are revealed is arbitrary. Berkeley attempts to supply such a premise with his discussion of animals with microscopic eyes.[8] Microscopes and, according to Berkeley, eyes come with a variety of resolving powers. At each resolution the same object may present a different color appearance. It seems completely arbitrary which viewing conditions we pick as the ones that reveal the true color of the object. Russell also makes a similar point when he asks, "If, then, we cannot trust what we see with the naked eye, why should we trust what we see through a microscope?" We have no reason to select any one of the various colors an object may appear to possess as its true color. We seem forced to conclude with Berkeley that "all colors are equally apparent and that none of those which we perceive are really inherent in any outward object."[9]

It may seem as if this addition to the argument from microscopes is really quite dubious. For there is an epistemologically

[8]Berkeley, *Three Dialogues*, p. 25.

[9]Strictly speaking, the conclusion should be that we have no way of perceptually determining true color, not that there is no such thing. Objectivists about color, however, will not be attracted by the view that external objects are objectively colored although we have no perceptual access to such colors.

privileged set of conditions, what is sometimes called normal conditions. The drop of blood is really red because that is the appearance it exhibits in normal conditions, i.e., to the naked eye. Normal conditions are privileged because what we mean by the real color of an object is that color it appears to possess when viewed in normal conditions. This line of attack on Berkeley's argument makes too much of concession to the argument, however, and there are other problems with the argument from microscopes that do not depend on singling out an epistemologically privileged set of viewing conditions or make the real color of an object conceptually dependent on the conditions under which it is viewed. This objection to Berkeley's argument also fails to appreciate the force of the considerations raised by Berkeley about animals with different types of eyes. There are serious problems raised about the objectivity of colors by the possibility that some organisms may see colors differently from the way in which humans do. These problems are, however, separable from the argument from microscopes and will be discussed later.

In any event, the conclusion of the argument from microscopes itself is unacceptable. If we accept this conclusion, we must either suppose that our scientific instruments convey information about the micro-structure of blood drops by producing color illusions (supposing that they do convey such information) or that almost all our color perceptions are illusory. Neither conclusion is fully compatible with our common-sense views on colors; it is worth seeing what can be said in favor of our reluctance to accept either conclusion. Also, it is not just microscopes that raise these problems. The sort of cases to which the argument from microscopes applies are a familiar feature of everyday life. We are not ordinarily puzzled by such cases and we are right not to be.

The first point to be made about the argument from microscopes is that one of its premises (P_4) is false. It is not true that "The drop of blood which appears red to the naked eye, and red and transparent through the microscope, is (identically) one and the same object." When we examine the drop of blood with the naked eye, we are seeing the color of the drop. When we look at the drop through the microscope, we are seeing the color of (some) of its parts. Although the drop is nothing more than the sum of its parts, it is not identical with its parts (taken singly or collectively). P_4 is false because it mistakenly asserts that the drop of blood is identical with that collection of its parts that we see through the microscope.

To make this point somewhat clearer, let us look at a new example that displays the same supposed conflict of appearance without resorting to the use of a microscope. If we look at a piece of cloth woven from red and white threads from a distance, it will appear to be pink. If we look at it from closer up it will appear to be composed of red and white threads. It is not the case that the cloth as a whole ever appears to be red and white. It is also not the case that the threads from which it is woven ever appear to be pink. When we look at the cloth from a distance we see the color of the cloth as whole. When we examine it from closer up we see the color of some of its parts, the threads from which it is woven. When we look at the cloth from a distance we cannot see the color of the threads and from close up we cannot see the color of the whole. Since the cloth is not identical with the threads from which it is woven, there is no conflict of appearances to which P_2 (the exclusion principle) could apply.

One response to this objection is to replace the exclusion principle with a stronger principle, one that will assert that a thing cannot be differently colored from its parts. This response is made by Armstrong in *Perception and the Physical World*. He considers the objection to the argument from microscopes just raised and asks: "It might be suggested here that there is no difficulty in saying that a drop of blood is *really* red, or at any rate, portions of a drop of blood are really red, and yet also saying that *very minute* portions have a different colour, or have no colour at all. A man is rational, but his hand is not rational. Why could not the same be true of the redness of drops of blood?"[10]

His response is a statement of what I will call the dissectivity principle. The name for this principle is taken from Nelson Goodman who points out that certain predicates have the property of being *dissective*. According to Nelson Goodman, "A one-place predicate is said to be *dissective* if it is satisfied by every part of every individual that satisfies it. Since every part of everything that is smaller than Utah is also smaller than Utah, the predicate 'is smaller than Utah' is dissective."[11] What I am calling the dissectivity principle asserts that color predicates are dissective in Goodman's sense. In replying to the objection raised above, Armstrong states a somewhat modified form of the dissectivity principle. He claims that "Although the parts of a (rational) man are not rational, the (coloured) parts of a coloured thing or coloured

[10]Armstrong, *Perception and the Physical World*, New York: Routledge & Kegan Paul, 1961, p. 162.
[11]Nelson Goodman,, *The Structure of Appearance*, Boston: D. Reidel, 1977, p. 53.

surface must be coloured all over."[12] In applying his analysis to Berkeley's example of the drop of blood, however, it is clear that he has the full-blown dissectivity principle in mind. He argues that "If a drop of blood really is red, then it is red *all over*, or proper parts of the drop are red *all over*. These parts cannot simultaneously be another colour, or be colourless. So the new colours, or lack of colour, revealed when a drop of blood is scrutinized under a microscope, are actually *incompatible* with the appearance presented to the naked eye. There is a conflict of appearances here, and at least one of the colour-perceptions *must* involve illusion."[13]

Appeals to the dissectivity principle concede the falsity of P_4 in my reconstruction of the argument from microscopes. What is being suggested is that we replace P_2 (the exclusion principle) with:

$P_{2'}$ The parts of a colored thing must be both colored all over and the same color as the thing itself (the dissectivity principle).

We must also replace P_4 with

$P_{4'}$ The drop of blood which appears red to the naked eye and that which appears red and transparent through the microscope stand in the relation of whole to part.

The argument from microscopes with these amendments is still valid and the objection raised above seems to have been answered. The crucial move is the replacement of the exclusion principle by the dissectivity principle. This replacement allows a defender of the argument of microscopes to accept the objection to P_4 while still maintaining that the argument poses a threat to the objectivity of colors.

The key to the argument from microscopes as reformulated is the dissectivity principle. It is important to point out how little support this principle gets from common sense. The facts the argument from microscopes relies on are ones we are all familiar with, but these facts do not lead us to conclude that many of our color perceptions are illusory. We seem to be quite comfortable with the idea that a thing may be composed of parts that differ in color from the thing itself. We do say things like, "That piece of pink cloth is woven from red and white threads." Such a statement does not carry any implication that the piece of cloth is not in fact pink or that the threads are not red and white.

[12]Armstrong, *Perception and the Physical World*, p. 162.
[13]Ibid., pp. 162–163.

Not all philosophers have found the dissectivity principle obvious. Goodman, for example, does not think that color predicates are dissective. He claims that:

> Different perceptible parts of an object may be differently colored even if the object itself is uniform and unvarying in color. This is no more paradoxical than the fact that a single object contains spatio-temporally different parts. As the self-identical object is a function of its parts, so the single unchanging color of the object is a function of the colors of its parts. The nature and interrelation of the lesser elements that make up the whole determine what kind of thing the whole is: the kind and arrangement of the colors exhibited by these various parts determine what color the whole is said to have.[14]

Goodman is not upholding the objectivity of colors in the way in which I am. He does not, however, find the failure of dissectivity for color predicates unintelligible or even, apparently, puzzling.

The dissectivity principle quite clearly conflicts with our common sense view of colors. I will not be able to argue conclusively that it is false. I will, however, attempt to point to some considerations that at least make the principle's falsity likely and to give some explanation of why Armstrong might find it a plausible principle. First, any argument based on the fact that no object ever presents more than one color appearance at a time has succumbed to an important fallacy. One of the fundamental tenets of anthropocentric realism is that what we are able to perceive in a given context depends not only on what is there to be perceived but also on the character of our perceptual systems. Our perceptions never provide us with complete information about the properties of the objects we are perceiving. They also may provide only partial information about determinates lying under some particular determinable. Vision provides partial information about objects, not only in the sense that there are properties that are not visually accessible, but also in the sense that even properties that are visually accessible may not be completely determined by any given visual perception. Our perception of the world is often partial, and to assume that perception gives us total information about any property is to commit what I call the fallacy of total information.

The fallacy of total information in the form relevant to the argument from microscopes is the assumption that if an object's color is perceived at all, then every aspect of its color must be perceived in complete detail. An argument for the truth of the exclusion principle that commits this fallacy may make the point somewhat clearer. The exclusion principle prohibits any area of an object from having two incompatible colors. It is tempting to argue that the exclusion principle must be true because no object is ever perceived to have more than one incompatible color at a time. To assume that if it is impossible to perceive an object to have two or more incompatible colors at the same time, then it is impossible that the object actually have two or more colors is to commit the fallacy of total information. The impossibility of perceiving an object to have more than one color at a time by itself implies nothing about the possibility of the object actually being multiply colored. It is perfectly consistent to claim both that we never see an object to have two different colors at the same time and that objects are actually multiply colored. The partial nature of our perception makes it possible that states of affairs that are perceptually incompatible are realized in fact.

It is important to distinguish this emphasis on the selective nature of perception from a claim that perception only reveals relational properties.[15] If the exclusion principle were false in the way I have been supposing, it would not be because color is a relation between object and perceiver. The relevant possibility is that color is a property such that objects are able to instantiate multiple colors at the same time. The relation between the perceiver and the object determines which of these many colors are perceptible in a given set of circumstances but not which colors the object actually possesses. Which properties we are able to perceive depends not only on what there is and what kind of creatures we are, but also on the circumstances in which we are perceiving.

Although the fact that we never perceive an object to be red and green all over does not imply that objects cannot be red and green all over, this fact is relevant to an investigation of the possibility of the co-occurrence of colors. The fallacy of total information consists in assuming that all we need is the perceptual impossibility to establish the actual impossibility. The exclusion principle is in fact true and the perceptual truths we have been discussing are part of the evidence for its truth. On the account of color I will

---

[15]My talk of the selective nature of perception is not meant as an endorsement of what is sometimes called the selective theory of perception. All I mean in claiming that perception is selective is that it does not reveal all aspects of all properties of external objects. Our perceptual systems are only capable of gathering information about some aspects of the manifold properties that objects possess. The selective theory of perception with its emphasis on unsensed sense data is a theory on a different level altogether. For the selective theory see H. H. Price, *Perception*, London: Methuen, 1950, pp. 40–54.

ultimately defend no object can possess two different determinate colors at the same time. Objects of different determinate colors have distinctive ways of interacting with light, among other things, and an object that had two different determinate colors would have physically incompatible interactions with the light which illuminates it. Part of the evidence for these differences in physical interactions is the effects differently colored objects have on human perceivers. These differences are not the only evidence and, unbuttressed by a theory of the physical nature of color would be insufficient to establish the exclusion principle.

We are now ready to return to my real target in this discussion: the dissectivity principle. One possible line of argument for the truth of the dissectivity principle is analogous to the argument discussed above for the truth of the exclusion principle. Unlike the exclusion principle, however, we will see that there are no alternative considerations that support the truth of the dissectivity principle. As we discovered in the preceding discussion, the mere fact that I am unable to see the pink color of the cloth as a whole at the same time that I am seeing the red and white color of the threads does not conclusively establish that the two color appearances are incompatible. To suppose that my perception of the cloth as a whole as pink conflicts with my perception of the threads as red and white without any other evidence is to subscribe to the fallacy of total information. Such a claim assumes that any given color appearance must deliver the whole truth about the object's color.

If we fail to make a pair of related distinctions this failure will make the perception of colors appear much more problematic than it actually is. The first distinction, discussed above, is that between an object and the parts of which it is composed. It is quite possible and quite common for the parts of an object to have properties significantly different from those of the object itself. Resting on this distinction is a distinction between seeing an object and seeing the parts of which it is made. When I look at a drop of blood I do not see the corpuscles and plasma of which it is composed. I am incapable of seeing red blood cells with my unaided eyes; the blood cells are just too small. I think Armstrong's argument derives its plausibility from an implicit assumption that in seeing the whole I must at the same time see the parts. In other words, the argument rests on the fallacy of total information. Armstrong (and Berkeley) seem to be assuming that when I see an object to be of a certain color, I have seen all there is to see about its color, even the color of its parts. It is important to notice that when I look at a drop of blood it is not the case that I see it as not having parts, rather I do not see the parts. Without a microscope I cannot tell anything at all about the parts which might compose a drop of blood, even whether there are any parts. If we could see all the parts of the drop of blood with our unaided eyes, we would have no need for microscopes. Objects would look just the same through a microscope as they do without it. For better or worse, our eyes have limited resolution and this limitation enables us to discover new facts about objects by getting closer to them or using optical aids: facts such as the colors of some of the object's parts.

The fallacy of total information, in the form I have been attributing it to Armstrong and Berkeley, involves a confusion between failing to perceive something and perceiving that something is not present. In the case of the pink cloth, the confusion is to infer from the fact that I do not see it to have red and white parts that I see its parts not to be red and white. It is a common feature of all our perceptual experiences that they do not specify all the aspects of the object perceived. Our perceptions are often indeterminate, a fact that will be of importance in a later chapter. As a result of this indeterminacy there is a very real difference between not perceiving that a certain object has a certain property and perceiving that the object does not have the property in question. It is a confusion of this sort that gives the dissectivity principle its plausibility.

I have been concentrating on the fallacy involved in assuming that if one sees the color of the whole one must also see the color of the parts. It is important to note that it is just as much of a fallacy to assume that in seeing the color of the parts of an object, even all of the proper parts, one thereby sees the color of the whole. If one sees the color of all of the proper parts of an object, one may (sometimes) be able to infer the color of the whole, but this does not entail that the object is seen (or appears) to have that color. In a more recent article Armstrong considers a reply to the argument from microscopes similar to the one I have been putting forward.[16] He rejects it on the grounds that even though the drop of blood is not identical with its parts, a "color map" of the drop built up from the colors of all its microscopic parts will display the necessary conflict with the apparent color of the whole drop. He asks us to imagine that:

> A microscope is deployed bit by bit over the whole of an area easily visible to the naked eye. A certain colour picture of the area could be

[16]Armstrong, "Colour Realism," pp. 107–109.

built up — it could be literally pictured on some much larger area — which will, in general, be incompatible with the colour appearances presented to the naked eye. Thus a drop of blood looks red all over to the naked eye, but a colour picture of the same drop obtained by deploying a microscope over the whole surface of the drop would not contain very much red.[17]

He thinks his argument is bolstered by imagining creatures with eyes having the resolving power of a microscope but the field of view of a human eye. Such a creature would see all of the drop of blood at one time but it would present the appearance to it that it presents to a human employing a microscope. He concludes that the two color patterns would be incompatible.

One way of construing this argument would have it relying on the dissectivity principle and merely taking a different approach to demonstrating the difference in color between the whole and the parts. Armstrong actually has something different in mind. His argument here seems to rely on identifying the color of the whole with a certain aggregate of its parts. He seems to be claiming that the color of the whole must be identical to the color obtained by making a map of the color of its parts, where each microscopic part is enlarged to visible size. It is almost certainly true, as Goodman points out, that the color of the whole is related to the color of its parts but there is no need for it to be the particular relation Armstrong settles on. Armstrong has assumed that if one sees the color of all the proper parts at once, one thereby sees the color of the whole. To make this assumption is once again to commit the fallacy of total information.

Perceptual properties in general do not obey the assumption Armstrong makes. A square thing may be composed of round parts. One may see all of the round parts and still not be able to *see* the square shape of the whole. It may be possible via an examination of the round parts to infer that the shape of the whole is square but it may not be possible to *see* that it is square. There is nothing particularly puzzling about this phenomenon. Similarly, with respect to the drop of blood one may be able to infer that the drop as a whole is red from an inspection of its various parts, but it may not be possible to see that it is red. There is no requirement that an object display all of its color properties from any given point of view. It may be possible to have the whole surface of the drop of blood visible at one time through a microscope. The drop may still fail to display its color. From such a point of view we can see the color of

[17]Ibid., p. 108.

the parts but not the color of the whole. The color of the drop as a whole is just not visible from that viewpoint. Similarly, it is sometimes impossible to determine the shape of a wall one is standing next to. All of the wall is visible yet one is still unable to see its shape. The wall is just too close to be able to determine its shape. Failing to see that an object has a certain property differs in important respects from seeing that an object lacks that property.

The argument from microscopes, then, depends on the truth of the dissectivity principle for its soundness. Dissectivity is not a universal property of predicates, and claims that predicates of a certain sort are dissective require justification. Armstrong's attempt to argue that color predicates are dissective commits the fallacy of total information and consequently fails to establish its conclusion. None of this establishes that colors are not dissective, however, and Armstrong makes a case for the compatibility of the dissectivity principle and objectivity with respect to colors. The objectivity that Armstrong claims for colors is of a rather limited sort. Since heterogeneity of color on the microscopic level is a common property of objects, most of our common ascriptions of particular colors to objects will turn out to be mistaken. In Armstrong's view colors are objective but unaided perception is a rather poor guide to the colors of things. I will not attempt to argue explicitly that the dissectivity principle is false, and with it Armstrong's analysis, but will instead offer an analysis of colors in which they will not be dissective. An explanation of the failure of dissectivity for colors in an account that is otherwise satisfactory should be sufficient to refute the dissectivity principle. Chapter 7 shows how the conceptual arguments advanced here fit in with the positive account of the nature of color that I develop. By rejecting the dissectivity, principle we avoid the need for heroic stratagems in the defense of color realism.

3

COLOR AND SCIENCE

THE NEXT SET of arguments that I will consider all take their inspiration from science. These arguments all make the claim that the structure of the world revealed to us by modern science has no place for color or the other secondary qualities. I will consider two examples of such arguments. The first, and probably the best known, makes use of the fact that the fundamental particles of physics are colorless. The description derived from physics of the world as composed of collections of discrete, colorless particles is held to be inconsistent with the common sense description of the world as composed of continuous and continuously colored objects. This argument, as I interpret it, attempts to show that the conceptual scheme of physics is inconsistent with the conceptual scheme of common sense. There is no place, it is claimed, in the conceptual structure of physics for color as we commonly conceive it. The second argument attempts to show that even if we allow that color *may* be a derivative and complex physical property, a careful analysis will show that it is not such a property. This argument attempts to show on empirical grounds that science leaves no room for color. It is not that color could not be compatible with physics, but rather that there is nothing in physics that corresponds to color as we experience it. The first argument can be dismissed on much the same grounds as the argument from microscopes. In discussing the second argument, we will get important insight into the true nature of color.

The first argument may be stated quite concisely. Jackson puts the argument into these two sentences: "Physics shows that objects are collections of minute, widely-separated, *colourless* particles.

Therefore, they are not coloured."[1] This argument may appear to be a version of the argument from microscopes and it is similar in important respects.   There is, however, one very important difference between this argument and the argument from microscopes, for the current argument makes no use of conflicting appearances. In the argument from microscopes we are confronted with a conflict between the way in which an object appears under differing conditions. The argument currently under consideration does not rely on perception at all. Instead it is claimed that the truth about the world, as revealed by physics, leaves no room for colors. Our color perceptions could be perfectly stable and consistent and it would not matter to this argument at all.

It is claimed, then, that there is a conflict between the common sense view of the world as consisting of colored external objects and the view given by physics of a world consisting of collections of colorless particles. The argument for such a conflict proceeds by way of an application of a variant of the dissectivity principle.   An example of such an argument is given by Bruce Aune. He claims that it is impossible that "a gappy collection of colorless particles" can be colored in the way that is required by common sense. His argument is that:

> If we attend . . . to the essential features of a material surface—to those features that place it in the category of material surfaces—we can see that these features must belong to every one of the surface's subregions, however small they may be. (Without these features, the regions would not count as sections of the surface.) Since color and tangibility are the essential features of a typical material surface, it thus follows that every subregion of such a surface, however minute, must have color and some species of tactile quality. But this kind of sensible continuity . . . cannot possibly characterize the surface layer of a gappy system of particles.[2]

The crucial premise in this argument is that every subregion of a material surface must have color. This claim is open to two interpretations and so presents Aune with a dilemma. If it is interpreted as a claim that every part of a surface must be colored, then the truth of this claim would lead to a conflict between common sense and physics. So interpreted, the premise is false. If by subregion of a material surface Aune means "a part of a material surface that is

---

[1]Jackson, *Perception*, p. 121. Jackson does not endorse the argument but does not refute it either.

[2]Bruce Aune, *Knowledge, Mind, and Nature*, New York: Random House, 1967, p. 172.

itself a material surface," then the truth of this claim would not by itself establish any conflict between common sense and physics.

The first claim, that every part of a material surface must be colored, is easily seen to be false. The fact that, as Aune claims, color is an essential property of material surfaces is irrelevant. There is no reason to suppose that every part of a material surface must itself be a material surface and, consequently, that every part of a material surface must be colored. This interpretation of Aune's claim is just a weakened form of the dissectivity principle. Aune is claiming that if something is colored then all of its parts must be colored. There is as little reason to suppose that this weakened form of the dissectivity principle is true as there was for the dissectivity principle itself. Although on this interpretation Aune's argument is valid, one of its crucial premises turns out to be false.

The other horn of the dilemma is to interpret Aune as claiming that every part of a material surface that is itself a material surface must be colored. On this interpretation, the phrase "subregion of a material surface" is taken to mean "part of a material surface that is itself a material surface." If Aune is right that being colored is an essential property of material surfaces, then it would certainly be true that all subregions of a material surface must be colored. This fact by itself, however, has no implication that there is a conflict between physics and common sense. What it will show is that the colorless particles of physics cannot be material surfaces in the sense of that term which requires that such surfaces be colored. Unless some justification is offered for concluding that all parts of a material surface must themselves be material surfaces, the argument fails to establish its conclusion.

Aune seems to imply that subregions of a surface may be made indefinitely small. If we allow that every subregion of a surface has to be colored and that subregions can be made as small as we like we are faced with a dilemma. Very small subregions of the surface may be composed either of a single particle or even empty space. We must either claim that something colored, i.e., a surface, exists where physics tells us there is only a colorless particle or nothing at all, or we must acknowledge that the existence of colored surfaces is incompatible with physics.

This dilemma vanishes, however, if we assume that colored surfaces have some minimum size. We may suppose that color is an emergent property of objects, one that is only found in objects that have attained a particular size and a particular structure.[3] If color is, in fact, a property that only attaches to objects that are big enough, then the supposition of Aune's argument is false. Colored surfaces are not divisible without limit into smaller colored surfaces. The minimum size that a colored surface must have may be considerably larger than the dimensions of the particles postulated by physics. Unless we suppose, unjustifiably, that the parts of a colored surface of minimum size must themselves be colored, there will be no conflict between science and common sense over colors.

The only reason for supposing that anything that is colored must be continuously colored is that our perceptions of color are not gappy. When we see a uniformly colored surface we do not see a field consisting of many individual domains of color. The inference from this fact to the claim that color must be continuously distributed over the surface is faulty. To suppose that the fact that we do not see the surface to be composed of individual, minimal color domains implies that such domains cannot exist is to commit the fallacy of total information. There is a difference between not seeing that an object has a particular property and seeing that an object does not have that property. There is nothing in our perception of color or in our common sense concept of color to imply that something that is colored must be capable of being divided indefinitely into other colored things.

There is no immediate conflict between attributing colors to physical objects and the physical sciences. It still may be argued, however, that there is no place for color in the physicist's view of the world. If we leave aside the view that color is an irreducible property of physical objects, we are left with the task of finding some derivative physical property that can be identified with color. Our task takes the form of finding some physical property that is shared by, for example, all and only blue things. It is this task that what I will call *the argument from wavelengths* attempts to show is impossible.

Before discussing the argument from wavelengths itself, I will first sketch the conception of the relation between color and physics in which it is embedded. This conception is essentially the one developed by Newton divorced from his subjectivist account of the color of light. The argument from wavelengths makes the same

[3]Armstrong considers such a possibility in discussing the argument from microscopes. He thinks the view is perfectly intelligible but does not constitute a reply to the argument. See Armstrong, *Perception and the Physical World*, p. 162.

assumptions as did Newton about the nature of colors and their relation to physics. These assumptions are partly based on well-known empirical facts about colors and light and partly based on the nature of our phenomenological experience of colors. Together these assumptions form a certain view of the possibilities open for a reductionist account of colors. These assumptions, as the argument from wavelengths shows, lead to the conclusion that no reductionist account of color is possible. I will call this conception of color, for reasons that will become apparent, *the wavelength conception of color*.

The first component of the wavelength conception of color is an assertion that information about color is carried by light. Another way of putting this is that the causal intermediary between a colored thing and our eyes is light. Color is in this sense an optical property. This assumption is very widely shared. The fact that color is somehow involved with light is an empirical fact that is understood by almost everyone, philosopher or not. It can be verified by simple experiments we can all perform. Switching off the lights in a room will destroy our ability to perceive the color of the objects in the room. Placing an opaque object in front of our eyes will also interfere with our ability to perceive the color of objects behind it. More sophisticated research also confirms the truth of this component of the wavelength conception of color. Light is an essential part of the causal chain leading to the perception of color. All the information that is available to visual perception is carried by properties of the light reaching the eyes of a perceiver. The information specifying colors is no exception.

The second component of the wavelength conception is that colors are always localized in space. Our experience of color is almost always of colored objects and surfaces. Even the blue of the sky seems to be the color of a thin film extending from horizon to horizon. The contrast here is with perceptual properties such as sounds and smells. Sounds, although often perceived as belonging to particular events, are also perceived to permeate space. In the case of odors the contrast is even clearer. Odors are not perceived to be localized spatially with respect to objects in the way colors are. Colors, on the other hand, are always perceived to be on the objects they belong to. A color typically occupies a more or less clearly defined place on the surface of an object.

This assumption is generally true. There are what are known as volume colors, colors that appear to qualify a volume rather than a surface. Typical examples are the colors of transparent or translucent objects. A glass of beer provides an example of a volume color.

In these cases the perceived color is still spatially localized. The color of a glass of beer is localized to the volume of the glass not just to the surface. Since these cases will not be important to the present argument I will restrict my discussion to surface colors.

These two components of the wavelength conception combine to yield the third and most important component. Taken together these two sets of facts lead to the conclusion that colors, if they are anything in objects at all, must be the power that an object has to reflect light of a given character. If we formulate this conclusion in terms of surfaces instead of objects, the assumption then becomes that the color of a surface is correlated with the character of the light reflected by that surface. From the fact that color is typically perceived to be a property of spatially delimited surfaces and that perception of color is causally mediated by some property of light, we infer that perceived color must be correlated with the character of the light reaching the eye from that surface.

The argument underlying this conclusion is quite simple. The first premise is our first fact about colors, namely, that perception of color is causally mediated by some property of light. Another way of putting this is that the immediate external correlate of perceived color is some property of the light at the eye. Our second premise is that colors are spatially localized. From these two premises it seems to follow that the perceived color of a surface must be correlated with some localized property of the light at the eye. Since colors are perceived to be on the surfaces of objects it is the light reaching the eye from the surface in question that must be correlated with the perceived color of that surface. We have reached our conclusion: the perceived color of a surface is correlated with some property of the light reaching the eye from that surface. I will call this conclusion *the local light assumption*.

This conclusion is a very important part of many philosophers' conception of the connection between perceived color and the physical world. For example, many philosophers (and other people as well) believe that perceived color is correlated with the wavelength of the light reaching the eye from a colored surface. This view is a special case of the local light assumption. It is a proposal for the unspecified property of light with which colors are supposed to be correlated. The proposal that colors are to be correlated with wavelengths of light has been, and still is, very influential in thinking about colors. An example of a philosopher who held such a view is Russell. In *Human Knowledge: Its Scope and Limits* he makes the following claims. "Let us suppose that I am seeing a certain colored patch, and that I call the shade of the patch 'C'. Physics tells me that this shade of color is caused by light of wave length L. I may then define 'C'. . . . as the shade of any visual sensation caused by electromagnetic waves of wave length L; or as electromagnetic waves of wave length L."[4] This view of the physical correlate of color is very popular and has been shared by many psychologists as well as philosophers.

The wavelength conception of colors has several consequences and among these is the instability of color. The local light assumption implies that perceived color will vary with changes in illumination. More accurately the local light assumption in conjunction with the empirical fact that the character of the light reflected by a surface is dependent on the character of the light illuminating the surface implies that perceived color will vary with illumination. If we claim that perceived color is correlated with properties of the light reaching the eye from a surface, then we are committed to claiming that perceived color is illumination dependent. The character of the light reaching the eye from a surface is jointly determined by properties of the surface and the character of the light that illuminates the surface. A corollary of the supposed illumination dependence of color is that perceived color will be changed by looking through a color filter. Interposing a filter between a surface and the eye is one way of changing the character of the light reaching the eye from an object. On the local light assumption any such filter will produce a change in perceived color.

This consequence has been, for the most part, embraced by philosophers. Ayer, for example, speaks of "the continuous alteration in the apparent colour of an object which was seen in a gradually changing light."[5] C.I. Lewis also apparently shared this view. He claims that "color, as perceived, varies with illumination. Except in light of *some* candle-power color cannot be seen at all, but the perceptual content itself varies with variation of the candle-power."[6] Philosophers have also accepted the corresponding result with regard to filters. It is a well-known piece of philosophical lore that persons suffering from jaundice see objects to be more yellow than normal perceivers. The supposed dependency of perceived color on illumination has played a part in many argu-

[4]Russell, *Human Knowledge: Its Scope and Limits*, New York: Simon and Schuster, 1948, p. 261.

[5]A.J. Ayer, *The Foundations of Empirical Knowledge*, New York: St. Martins Press, 1962, p. 8.

[6]C.I. Lewis, *Mind and the World Order*, New York: Dover Publications, 1929, p. 171.

ments attempting to establish that color cannot be a property of material things. Other philosophers have supposed that a correct analysis of color must include a specification of "normal" conditions, including a precise specification of the intensity and character of the illumination.

Another consequence of this conception is the argument from wavelengths itself. The argument from wavelengths takes its premises from this conception of color. As I will show, the argument from wavelengths is valid, and granted the accuracy of the conception of color as wavelength dependent, the argument does establish that there is no possible reductive analysis of color. This conception of color is flawed, however, and some of the premises of the argument from wavelengths must be rejected. A discussion of this argument will help to make clearer the nature of these flaws and will point to a solution of the difficulties raised for the objectivity of colors by the conception of colors as characterized in terms of local properties of light.

Versions of the argument from wavelengths have been offered by many philosophers. Perhaps the most famous version of the argument is the one used by Smart to argue for a behaviorist theory of colors.[7] The version of the argument I will consider is given by Campbell.[8] Campbell's version of the argument shares its essential features with Smart's and has the virtue of being considerably more detailed. They both think that the argument establishes that if colors are correlated with any physical property at all that the property must be an implausibly complex and disjunctive one. It is only fair to Campbell to mention now that in a later paper he refutes his own argument for reasons related to the ones I will offer.[9] The argument is still influential, however, and discussing it will

[7]Smart gives the argument in several places. Among them are *Philosophy and Scientific Realism*, London: Routledge & Kegan Paul, 1963, p. 69– 72, and "Colours," pp. 131–134.

[8]Campbell, "Colours," in *Contemporary Philosophy in Australia*, edited by R. Brown and C. D. Rollins, pp. 132–157.

[9]Campbell, "The Implications of Land's Theory of Colour Vision,"in *Logic, Methodology, and Philosophy of Science: Vol. 6*, edited by L. J. Cohen, pp. 541–552. Although Campbell disavows the argument from wavelengths in light of the experimental results to be described in the next chapter he still remains a subjectivist about color. His argument for subjectivism relies on a form of Locke's thesis of the lack of resemblance between perceptions of color and their physical ground. As we saw in Chapter 1, however, the resemblance thesis does not support a conclusive argument against the objectivity of color.

help us in avoid the flaws of the conception of color from which the argument derives.

Before discussing Campbell's argument, I will place a limitation on the range of color phenomena under consideration. Psychologists interested in color vision have distinguished a number of modes of color appearance.[10] They may be classed into three main categories: illumination, film, and object modes. These categories may be further subdivided. Illumination colors are those that are perceived as properties of the illumination. An example of a film color is the color seen through a spectroscope or the blue of the day sky. Object colors, which will be my primary interest, are those that are perceived as attributes of an object. In the particular case where it is the surface of the object that is perceived as the bearer of color, these are called surface colors. Most of our color perceptions are of surface colors. A solution to the problems posed by surface colors will take us a long way to the solution of the problem of color in general. By limiting the range of discussion to surface colors, I will not evade any of the important points raised by Campbell.

The position Campbell takes himself to be arguing against is what he calls "reductive physical realism" about colors. He claims that:

> Proponents of objective doctrines of colour who wish to find a place for colours in the physicists' account of nature must hope to find some complex and derivative physical property common and peculiar to all those objects which are, say, turquoise. They must urge that associated with turquoise things there is indeed a distinctive pattern of effect upon other physical objects, although not a pattern different from any flowing from combinations of other qualities in the coloured item. They must urge further, that the colour of a turquoise surface can be identified with its common physical peculiarity, thus offering a *reductive* physical realism for colour.[11]

His strategy is to argue that there is no common physical peculiarity to all and only things that are seen to be turquoise. His argument depends on showing that there is a lack of adequate correlation between colors as perceived and any plausible physical candidate. If there is no plausible physical correlate for perceived color, then it is hard to see how a reductive physical analysis could succeed. The objectivist about color would have to maintain that

[10]My discussion of the modes of color appearance follows that of Jacob Beck, *Surface Color Perception*, Ithaca, NY: Cornell University Press, 1972, pp. 16–32.

[11]Campbell, "Colours," p. 136.

although colors are to be identified with a certain physical property the colors we see are not correlated with that property. Although colors are objective, in this view, most of our color perceptions would be illusory. A view such as this would seem to have very little to recommend it.

Campbell starts his argument by distinguishing between what he calls transitory and standing colors. He makes this distinction on the basis of the familiar fact that the perceived color of a surface can vary with changes in illumination. A surface that appears blue under one illumination may appear green under a different one. What Campbell calls transitory color is a relation between objects and illuminations. The transitory color of a surface is the color that surface has relative to a given illumination. The transitory color of a surface, thus, may vary with changes in illumination. This definition of transitory colors fits very nicely with the wavelength conception of color. In that conception colors are to be reduced to the powers of objects to reflect light of a particular character. This implies that objects will have different colors in different illuminations. Campbell points out that although transitory colors are relative properties, they may still be objective. Standing colors, on the other hand, are those colors that are constant under changes of illumination. According to Campbell, standing colors are assigned to objects by choosing a standard illumination. We take the transitory color an object has relative to the standard illumination and suppose that the color is a permanent feature of the object. It follows that we can define standing colors in terms of transitory ones. An object is *standing* blue if it is *transitory* blue in the standard illumination.

Campbell is inclined to identify transitory colors with the appearance a color presents to a normal observer in a given illumination. He makes claims such as "A transitory colour is a colour a surface now seems to have."[12] To make such an identification is to prejudge an important issue: the possibility of misperceiving transitory colors. There are four concepts that need to be kept separate. In addition to transitory and standing colors, we also need apparent and real colors. Apparent (or perceived) colors are the colors a normal perceiver would perceive an object to have in the given circumstances. An object's real color, as I will understand it, is the color the object has independently of how it is perceived. These concepts need not differ in their extensions. It might turn out that Campbell is correct in assuming that the apparent color of an object

[12]Ibid., p. 134.

varies in the same way as its transitory color. This assumption is built into the conception of color he is using. It also might turn out that there is no such thing as an object's real color as I am using the term. If the argument from wavelengths were to be successful, it would be very misleading to talk of the object's color independently of how it is perceived. Since colors would lack physical correlates, the question of what color a given object has would be decidable only by appealing to the color it is perceived to have. For now, I only wish to emphasize that there are these four distinct concepts and that to confuse them is to beg important questions.

Campbell claims that transitory colors are conceptually prior to standing colors. This claim is certainly true for standing colors as he conceives them. There is another concept of standing color that is suggested by some of the things Campbell says, but that does not accord with his final analysis. The fundamental feature of standing colors is that they are constant under change of illumination. Campbell supposes that to achieve this constancy we identify the standing color of an object with its transitory color under the standard illumination. We might, however, suppose that objects have illumination-independent colors without supposing that these colors are to be defined in terms of transitory colors. It is just a truth about the object that it is that particular color. In this conception of color unlike the wavelength conception, there will be no obvious place for transitory colors. We can still define transitory color as Campbell does but, if we keep clear the distinction between transitory and apparent color, there will be no connection between this notion and any of the other concepts of color discussed above. If we take this alternate conception of standing color, there may be no interesting color property that is illumination dependent.

It is important to keep the distinction between transitory and apparent colors clear for it may appear that I am suggesting an epistemological impossibility. I am not claiming that the color an object appears to have at a given viewing is epistemologically secondary to the color it has independently of the circumstances of viewing. Obviously, all our immediate perceptual knowledge of the colors of objects comes via their apparent colors. What I am claiming is that standing colors can be conceived to be ontologically independent of any color property that is relative to illumination. It is important to keep issues about how we know what color an object is conceptually separate from issues about the nature of color. The ontology and epistemology of colors are related but distinct topics.

An analogy may help make these issues somewhat clearer. We could define a property called transitory length. The transitory length of an object is a function of the size of the projection of the object on the retina of a normal observer. For concreteness, let us suppose that the transitory length of an object is measured by holding a ruler four inches in front of the observer's face and parallel to the observer's facial plane. An object will have a transitory length of four inches if and only if the projection of its ends lie four inches apart on such a ruler. The transitory length of an object is just the length of its projection on a ruler positioned as described. Transitory length, defined as above, is a relation between an object and its position in relation to the observer. The transitory length of an object will vary as the distance of the observer from the object varies and also as the object is viewed from different angles. We can also define standing length on the basis of transitory length. The standing length of an object is the transitory length it has in standard circumstances. Standard circumstances are defined by choosing some particular relative position. Standing length will be a permanent property of objects.

The analogy between transitory lengths and transitory color should be obvious. Both take a given perceptual property to be essentially relational and both take whatever non-relational versions of the property there are to be defined in terms of the relational property. Standing length is dependent on transitory length in just the same way as standing color is dependent on transitory color. In the case of length, however, I think it is clear that our concept of an object's length is not the concept of standing length defined above. We conceive of the length of an object as an observer independent property of the object. Proper choice of the conditions that define standing length can make the standing length of an object always equal to ordinary length. This fact does not establish that standing length is the appropriate analysis of our ordinary concept of length. Standing length is dependent on transitory length in a way that our ordinary concept of length is not. It is also important to notice that the apparent length of an object has little to do with its transitory length. In most circumstances, objects do not appear to change in length as we change our position relative to them. Whatever the explanation for the phenomena of size constancy, it is clear that there is as little connection between perceived length and transitory length as there is between our ordinary concept of length and standing length.

The wavelength conception of color makes color fit Campbell's scheme with transitory color primary and standing color secondary.

What I want to suggest is that there may be an alternative conception of colors that assimilates them to the way we commonly conceive lengths. On this conception, colors are illumination-independent properties of objects. Objects are colored in the same way as they have lengths. These colors are not dependent on a relational concept of color. Also, on this conception, it need not be the case that the apparent colors of objects vary in the way transitory colors do. I will develop this alternative to the wavelength conception of colors below. For now it is only necessary to keep these issues in mind as I discuss the argument from wavelengths.

The structure of Campbell's argument is fairly simple. First he argues that the important question for the tenability of an objectivist view of colors has the form, "Is there any common peculiarity of the light by which turquoise, olive or magenta objects are respectively seen?"[13] The view of color for which this question is crucial is one that identifies colors with dispositional properties of objects to reflect light of a particular character. In this view, "For object O to be of transitory colour C_n is for O to have the power so to modify the incident light that the light O reflects has a composition characteristic for C_n objects."[14] This view of color is just the one entailed by the wavelength conception of colors. He then argues that the search for some common peculiarity of the light by which objects of a particular color are seen must be conducted among the wavelength and intensity characteristics of that light. The final step of the argument is to establish that there is no characteristic wavelength and intensity distribution associated with all and only objects of any particular perceived color. The crucial step in this argument is the first one, establishing that any reductive analysis of color must be in terms of properties of the light reflected. As we have seen, this amounts to establishing that the wavelength conception of colors is correct. Once this premise is granted, the conclusion that any reductive physical account of color is impossible follows quite easily.

Campbell starts his argument for this premise by pointing out that, since color is a visual phenomenon, the obvious place to search for a physical correlate is in properties of light and those properties of objects that affect their interaction with light. He goes on to point out that the physical causes of color in objects, even surface colors, are quite various. An object may appear blue, for example, from at least two causes. Some blues are the result of selective ab-

[13]Ibid., p. 139.
[14]Ibid., p. 138.

sorption of the incident light by a pigment. Other blues, known as structural blues, are the result of the microstructure of the surface of the object. They appear blue because short wavelengths are more likely to be backscattered than long wavelengths. The sky appears blue for a similar reason.[15] These considerations lead to the conclusion that blue objects have in common, at most, a certain characteristic transformation of the incident light. If there is to be any physical correlate of color, it must be a dispositional property of objects, their power to transform the composition of the light striking them.

There is a well-known dispositional property of objects that corresponds to the power to transform the light striking an object. This is the *surface spectral reflectance* of an object. The surface spectral reflectance of an object specifies the percentage of the incident light at each wavelength that is reflected by the object. To measure the surface spectral reflectance of a given point on the surface of an object the ratio of the flux of incident light to the flux of reflected light is measured for each wavelength. Surface reflectances, thus conceived, are stable properties of objects. Leaving photosensitive surfaces aside, the reflectance of an object is independent of illumination. The intensity and wavelength of the light reaching any given point is given by the *spectral power distribution* of the light. The spectral power distribution of a light describes the energy per second at each wavelength. It is easy to see from these definitions that the spectral power distribution of the light reaching the eye from a given point is jointly fixed by the spectral power distribution of the light incident on that point and the surface spectral reflectance of that point. In fact the spectral power distribution of the light reaching the eye from a given point is the product of the surface spectral reflectance with the spectral power distribution of the incident light.

Given these facts there are two main options for a possible physical correlate of color. We can investigate the possibility that colors are correlated with surface spectral reflectances. Or, and this is the position Campbell investigates, we can consider correlating individual colors with the complex property of having a surface spectral reflectance such that the spectral power distribution of the reflected light is characteristic of that color. The first option will make color a stable, illumination-independent property

---

[15]For a discussion of the various mechanisms underlying the light reflecting properties of surfaces see Kurt Nassau, *The Physics and Chemistry of Color*, New York: John Wiley & Sons, 1983.

of the object. The second option only makes sense if we are working within the wavelength conception of colors. This option also makes transitory colors primary. Since the spectral power distribution of the reflected light is the joint product of the surface reflectance and the spectral power distribution of the ambient light, the spectral power distribution of the reflected light will vary with illumination. An object with a constant surface reflectance will reflect light of a different spectral power distribution with every change in the character of the illumination. If we could correlate perceived color with the spectral power distribution of the reflected light, then Campbell would be right about the primacy of transitory colors. Perceived colors would be constantly changing under changing illumination.

Campbell offers little in the way of argument for conducting his search for the physical correlate of color among properties of light rather than properties of surfaces. We have seen, however, that this approach is the one that follows from the wavelength conception of colors. Colors are identified with the power to reflect light of a particular nature. It will be instructive to examine the consequences of adopting this conception of color. Adopting the wavelength conception of color we find that "The question: 'Can colours be given a place in the physicists' account of nature?' now takes the form: 'Are all and only blue objects seen by light characterized by some composition-and-intensity formula?'"[16] In our terminology this question becomes "Is there some spectral power distribution that is characteristic of the light reflected by blue objects."

Campbell argues that the answer to the question "Are all and only blue objects seen by light characterized by some composition-and-intensity formula?" is "No." His reason is that the state of adaptation of the eye is an additional factor that enters into the determination of perceived color. Exposure to predominantly red light for a period of time, for example, will cause the perceived color of objects looked at subsequently to have their perceived color shifted towards the blue-green. The same surface in the same illumination can appear, depending on the adaptive state of the observer, to have different colors at different times.

These facts appear to imply that there can be no physical characteristic of the surface that can be correlated with its transitory color. Suppose that we had a candidate for the physical correlate of blue. This correlate would have to be some characteristic spectral power distribution of the light reflected by

---

[16]Campbell, "Colours," p. 141.

objects that are transitory blue. The phenomena of adaptation show, however, that objects reflecting light with this spectral power distribution will not always appear to be blue. Adaptation can also lead objects with different spectral power distributions to appear blue. These facts show that there is no characteristic spectral power distribution of the light reflected by objects that appear to be blue.

We still have to make the step from showing that there is no physical correlate for perceived blue to showing that there is no physical correlate for transitory blue. It still could be maintained that the formula characterizes transitory blue but that we occasionally misperceive transitory colors. If we avoid the identification of transitory with apparent color, this possibility remains open. In order to take this position, one must maintain that there is a non-arbitrary distinction between real and apparent colors. In particular, we must be able to fix on some particular adaptive state as the one that reveals the real transitory color of objects. If such a distinction cannot be upheld, then the identification of transitory colors with physical properties is pointless. In the lack of such a distinction, transitory colors so identified would be epistemologically inaccessible to us. They would make no difference to our color experience.

Campbell addresses this point by arguing that any distinction between real and apparent colors must be arbitrary and based on factors external to the object itself. The difficulty he points to is that there is nothing in the physics to show which color an object reflecting light of a given spectral power distribution should have. It is only based on our color experiences that we can say which color an object with such a correlate should have. There is nothing in the physics of light that can tell us that an object reflecting predominantly long wavelength light is red as opposed to blue. He points out that in order to associate given patterns of light with colors we need to choose some adaptive state as the one that reveals the true color of things. To make such a choice involves determining the color of objects on grounds having nothing to do with the physical circumstances of objects. His argument, then, is that there is nothing in the nature of the object itself that allows us to distinguish between its real and apparent colors. Fixing a particular adaptive state as revealing the real color is to make an arbitrary distinction not based on anything in the object. The conclusion is that the failure to find any characterization of the spectral power distribution of the light reflected by a given object that correlates with the perceived color of that object shows that there is no possible physical correlate of transitory color.

I will not discuss Campbell's argument against the possibility of distinguishing between real and apparent colors now. This argument is just as relevant to the alternative to the wavelength conception of colors proposed in the next chapter as it is to the wavelength conception itself. The important issue is degree of correlation and not the arbitrariness of fixing on one state of the perceiver as revealing the true color of an object. There is even stronger evidence than Campbell puts forward to show that perceived color is not correlated with the spectral power distribution of the light reflected by an object. I will discuss this evidence below.

I have argued in this chapter that there is no conflict between the conceptual scheme of science and our ordinary conception of colors. The argument given by Aune and others to attempt to establish such a conflict between common sense and science fails for much the same reasons as did the argument from microscopes. Both these arguments rely on versions of the dissectivity principle and do not succeed for that reason. The failure of Aune's argument leaves open the possibility of a reductive analysis of colors. If there is no conceptual difficulty with reconciling physics and colors, we may be able to find some complex physical property with which colors can be identified.

The wavelength conception of colors offers a framework within which to look for such a physical property. This conception makes use of certain empirical facts about colors and color perception to underwrite a proposal as to what the physical property identified with colors must be like. On this conception of color, colors are to be identified with the dispositional property of objects to reflect light of a characteristic kind. For an object to be blue, on this conception, is for it to reflect the sort of light characteristic of blue objects.

The wavelength conception of color is not satisfied by colors as they are perceived. The argument from wavelengths establishes that there is no characteristic composition of the light reflected by objects that appear to be blue. The argument from wavelengths takes its premises from the wavelength conception of color. If we adopt the wavelength conception of color, then there is no physical reduction of color possible. The search for a physical property with which to identify color fails on empirical grounds. The facts about color do not allow for a reduction of color to some physical property within the constraints imposed by the wavelength conception of color. This failure presents us with a dilemma. We must either accept that color has no objective basis in physics, or we must give up the wavelength conception of color. In the next chapter I will argue that we should abandon the wavelength conception of color, and that doing so will enable us to succeed in our search for a physical correlate of color.

4

Color and Reflectance

THE ARGUMENT FROM wavelengths shows that if we adopt the wavelength conception of color there is no physical correlate of color. This conception of color, however, is not the only one available. My task now is to point out some of the flaws in the wavelength conception of color and show how these flaws lead us to a new conception of color. This conception of color will take color to be a permanent property of surfaces. Once we take the point of view that color is an illumination-independent property of objects, we are led to a new candidate for a physical correlate of color. This candidate is surface spectral reflectance.

I will start my discussion with an aspect of color vision that has been neglected by philosophers: color constancy. Philosophers, including Campbell, have been prone to make much of the supposed variability in color vision. Now it is certainly true that some changes in illumination can lead to changes in the color a surface is perceived to have. We are all familiar with the subtle effects some forms of fluorescent lighting can have on perception of greens and blues. Highly chromatic illuminations can produce quite startling changes in perceived color. We are also familiar with the changes in perceived color that can be induced by placing a filter, say colored spectacles, between a surface and the eye. A highly saturated filter can cause objects viewed through it to take on the color of the filter. We have seen that this variability is just what one would expect given the wavelength conception of colors.

What is less widely acknowledged, but should be equally familiar, is that in many circumstances changes in illumination lead to no change in perceived color. The illumination of an outdoor scene can vary widely depending on the time of day and the

61

atmospheric conditions. In spite of this our perception of the colors in such scenes is remarkably stable. Grass invariably appears green and for the most part the same area of a lawn will appear the same shade of green throughout the day. Although philosophers make much of the changes in perceived color due to fluorescent light they seem to have been much less aware of the fact that objects generally appear to have the same color under incandescent lamps that they do out of doors. Wearing an ordinary pair of sunglasses does not, in most circumstances, impair ones ability to identify the normal colors of objects. These are all examples of the phenomenon psychologists call color constancy. Color constancy is one of the striking characteristics of human color vision and accounting for it has been one the enduring theoretical challenges faced by researchers in color vision.

A careful consideration of color constancy will show that any attempt to correlate surface color with the spectral power distribution of the light reflected from a surface is doomed to failure. This lack of correlation could be taken in two different ways. On the one hand, within the wavelength conception of color it could be taken as a striking demonstration of the failure of realist theories of color. On the other hand, it could be taken as demonstrating the falsity of the local light assumption and with it the wavelength conception of color. The existence of color constancy suggests that perceived color is correlated with some property of the surfaces of objects and consequently that the wavelength conception of color is misguided. I will argue that the local light assumption is false and that the argument for its truth rests on a fallacy. Since the evidence for color constancy I have introduced so far is somewhat anecdotal, I will describe an experiment by Land that demonstrates some of the robustness of human color vision.[1] This experiment will also demonstrate that in viewing scenes of

---

[1]In spite of the long history of discussion of human color constancy in the psychological literature, there is surprisingly little in the way of experimental results giving precise descriptions of its extent and limits in ordinary viewing situations. The experiment of Land's that I will describe does not fill this gap. Land's experiment is a striking demonstration of the independence of perceived color from the spectral power distribution of the light reaching the eye from an object but does not contribute much to determining the precise nature of human color constancy. What is indisputable is that human color vision displays a substantial degree of constancy but its limitations and the factors involved are not well understood except in very special circumstances.

moderate complexity there is no correlation between perceived color and the spectral power distribution of the light reflected from a colored surface.

The apparatus for Land's experiment consists of two identical Color Mondrians, two sets of independently controllable slide projectors equipped with band-pass filters, and a telescopic photometer.[2] A Color Mondrian is a large array ($\approx$ 100 papers) of colored rectangular papers. Papers of any given color will appear several times in the array, each time with different neighbors and different shapes and sizes. There are three projectors for each Mondrian: one equipped with a filter passing only long wavelength light, one with a middle-wave filter, and one with a short-wave filter. The output of each projector is independently controllable. The photometer is capable of measuring the flux from any of the areas of the Mondrians.

A description of one type of experiment done with this apparatus will be sufficient for our purposes. The Mondrian on the left is illuminated by all three projectors and their output is adjusted so that the papers in the Mondrian appear deeply colored and the whites appear white. This setting is not critical. A paper from the array of some particular color, say white, is chosen from the Mondrian on the left and the photometer is aimed at it. All of the projectors except the long-wave one are turned off and the flux from the paper is measured. The procedure is repeated with the other two projectors so that a measure of the light reflected from the paper in each of the three wavebands is obtained. Next the photometer is aimed at a paper of a different color, say green, in the Mondrian on the right. Turning the projectors on one at a time, the output from each projector is adjusted so that the flux in each wave-band reflected from the green paper matches that from the paper in the Mondrian on the left. Finally, all three projectors are turned on at the same time. The paper on the right still appears green even though it is reflecting the same amount of light in each wave-band as was the white paper on the left. Similar results can be obtained with other pairs of colored papers. Two papers that reflect exactly the same amounts of light in each of the wavebands can have different perceived colors. Similarly, two papers that reflect different amounts of light in each of the three wavebands

[2]For a description of the experiments see Land, "The Retinex Theory of Color Vision," *Sci. Am.* 237, No. 6 (1977): pp. 108–128, and "Recent advance in retinex theory and some implications for cortical computations: Color vision and the natural image," *Proc. Natl. Acad. Sci. USA* 80 (1983): pp. 5163–5169.

can appear to have the same color. In general, the papers in each of the arrays match the papers in the other array that are physically similar in spite of the differences in the spectral power distribution of the light they are reflecting.

It is clear that this experiment decisively establishes the independence of perceived color from the spectral power distribution of the light reflected from a colored surface. Two surfaces reflecting light with the same spectral power distribution can have a different perceived color. At the same time, it shows that in the circumstances of Land's experiment, perceived color is independent of illumination. Changing illumination does not affect perceived color in the way that Campbell and other philosophers have supposed.

The fact that perceived color is not variable in the way that transitory colors are casts doubt on the wavelength conception of light. Recall that in the wavelength conception of light transitory colors were basic. This conception of light entailed that perceived color should be largely dependent on illumination. This illumination dependence was a consequence of the local light assumption: that information about the color of a surface must be carried in the light reaching the eye from that surface. The only aspect of light capable of carrying such information is its spectral power distribution. Since the spectral power distribution of the light reflected from a surface is jointly determined by the surface spectral reflectance of the surface and the spectral power distribution of the ambient light, the relevant characteristics of the light reaching the eye from that surface will vary with illumination.

The wavelength conception of color does not fit the empirical facts. The experiments of Land and others and our own experience show that perceived color in many circumstances is largely independent of wavelength.[3] If this independence took the form of arbitrary differences in the perceived color of objects reflecting light with the same spectral power distribution, then this would

[3]The failure of the wavelength conception was established experimentally well prior to the work of Land's that I discuss. The classic papers in the modern literature on the problem of predicting perceived color are Harry Helson, "Fundamental Problems in Color Vision. I. The principle Governing Changes in Hue, Saturation, and Lightness of Non-Selective Samples in Chromatic Illumination," *J. Exp. Psych.* 23, No. 5 (1938): pp. 439–476, and Deane B. Judd, "Hue, saturation and lightness of surface colors with chromatic illumination," *J. Opt. Soc. Am.* 30 (1940): pp. 2–32.

merely suggest that there is nothing in nature corresponding to perceived color. What we find instead is that there is a striking regularity in the excursions of perceived color from what would be expected on the basis of a wavelength analysis. Objects tend to retain their apparent color through changes in the character of the ambient light. The existence of color constancy should lead us to suspect the existence of some illumination-independent property of objects that is correlated with color. Perceived color in normal circumstances is illumination-independent and this suggests that we look for some illumination-independent physical correlate.

The obvious candidate for such a property is the one mentioned above: surface spectral reflectance.[4] The surface spectral reflectance of an object is, as described earlier, its disposition to reflect a certain percentage of the incident light at each wavelength. This property is an intrinsic, illumination-independent, property of the surface of an object. If color is surface spectral reflectance, then the fact that colors do not appear to change with changing illumination is explained. It might seem that the identification surface spectral reflectance with color meets the conditions that motivated the wavelength conception of light. These conditions, recall, were that color is spatially localized and that information about color must be embodied in light. Surface spectral reflectance is certainly spatially localized. Every part of surface will have its own surface spectral reflectance. Since the surface spectral reflectance of a surface partially determines the character of the light reaching the eye from that surface, it might seem that information about surface spectral reflectance is embodied in light in the right way.

[4]In spite of its obviousness there has been very little discussion of reflectance in philosophical work on color, even by writers defending physicalist theories of color. In addition to Campbell, two notable exceptions are Richard Grandy and Edward Averill. Grandy proposes that color is to be identified with reflectance but does not think an objectivist account of the reference of color language can be given in terms of reflectance. I will argue in Chapter 6 that such an account is possible. Averill defends a position similar in many respects to the one I defend. There are, however, significant differences of detail. Neither author makes the connection between modern theories of color vision and the traditional philosophical problems surrounding color. See Richard Grandy, "Red, white and blue? Stars and stripes? A modern inquiry into the physical reality of colors," unpublished ms., and Edward Averill, "Color and the Anthropocentric Problem," *J. Phil.* 82, No. 6 (1985): pp. 281–303.

There is a problem, however, with the compatibility of surface spectral reflectance and the requirement that information about color must be carried by light. To see the problem, consider a small area of a surface that has a uniform surface spectral reflectance and that is uniformly illuminated. This surface will reflect light that is focused on a particular area of the retina of the eye. The light that reaches the retina of the eye will not carry the information that the surface spectral reflectance has a particular value. The spectral power distribution of this light will be the product of the spectral power distribution of the ambient light with the surface spectral reflectance of the object. The light reaching the eye from this area of the surface cannot specify the reflectance of this area of the surface unless the illumination is known. These facts raise an apparent barrier towards identifying the color of a surface with its reflectance. It seems that, in the absence of knowledge of the illumination, there is no way to determine the reflectance of an object from the light it reflects. Colors so conceived would be epistemologically inaccessible.

The solution to these difficulties is to be found in an examination of the argument leading from our first two facts about color to the local light assumption. This argument has two premises: (1) perception of color is causally mediated by properties of light, and (2) that colors are spatially localized properties of surfaces. From this we concluded that the perception of the color of a surface must be causally mediated by the light reaching the eye from that surface. Another way of stating the local light assumption is that the information that specifies the color of the surface must be carried by the light reaching the eye from that surface. The two premises do not, however, imply the conclusion. It is possible that the overall character of the light reaching the eye determines the perceived color of each surface in the field of view. The argument in question ignores the possibility that the global character of the light available to the perceiver influences the effect produced by localized light of a given character.

What I am suggesting is that the local light assumption rests on a fallacy. This fallacy, *the fallacy of localization,* is what underlies the assumption that information about the color of a surface must be embodied in the light reaching the eye from that surface alone. What is being assumed is that information about a property that is spatially localized can only be carried via causal interactions with the particular area in which the property resides. In the case of color, the fallacy of localization amounts to assuming that the only part of the retinal stimulation that is relevant to determining the color of an object is that which originated with the object itself. The fallacy of localization improperly excludes contextual factors from consideration.

An example may help to make clearer both the nature of the fallacy of localization and the fact that it is a fallacy. Holograms are well-known examples of a medium in which the supposition of the fallacy of localization is quite clearly false. A hologram is a way of recording information about a three-dimensional scene in the form of interference patterns. Unlike a photograph a hologram is not formed by recording a projection of the scene on a two-dimensional surface. Holograms instead store information about the three-dimensional arrangement of objects in a scene in a form that is not geometrically similar to the spatial arrangement of the objects. Holograms are not images of the scenes they record. In this respect they differ from photographs in which the information about any particular part of the recorded scene has a definite spatial location and that information about spatial relation of parts of the scene is recorded in the form of spatial relations between parts of the hologram. If one asks about some part of a hologram projection where the information that specifies that part of the projection is located in the hologram, the answer is everywhere. The information about any part of the projected scene is stored in the overall pattern on the hologram. If one projects a part of a given hologram, one gets a degraded projection of the whole scene, not a projection of a part of the scene.[5] Holograms store their information in unlocalized form. They differ from ordinary photographs in this respect and they clearly display the fallacy involved in assuming that information that specifies a spatially localized property need be localized in the same way as the property. Information about the color of a surface may be carried in the overall pattern of light over the whole visual field just as information about some portion of a hologram projection is carried in the pattern of interference bands over the entire hologram.

Visual perception of spatial relations also provides examples of the failure of localization. The perception of depth for relatively near objects relies on comparing the information available to both

[5]"Each section of a hologram is capable of reconstructing an image of the entire object . . . Of course, a smaller portion of a hologram will reconstruct a correspondingly smaller section of the wavefront. If this portion is very small, the quality of the reconstructed image will become poorer, small details will vanish, and a characteristic speckled structure will appear." Ostrovsky, *Holography and its Application*, Moscow: Mir Publishers, 1977, p. 47.

eyes. If we focus on the information contained in the light reaching only one eye, then there is no way to obtain information about the distances of the objects in the field of view. It is only if we complicate our description of the stimulus that the information necessary to visually determine depth is available to the perceiver. There is also evidence to show that the visual perception of size is not determined solely by the size of retinal images of the various objects in the field of view. The relations between the sizes of the projections of objects onto the retina plays an important role in visual perception of size. Once again, the local stimulus is insufficient to explain the perceptual facts.

The fallacy of localization played an important part in the argument proposed in support of the local light assumption. It is only if we assume that information about the color of an object needs to be carried entirely by the light reflected from that object that we reach the conclusion that colors must be correlated with the character of that light. We can admit that colors are spatially localized and that information specifying color must be embodied in properties of the light reflected from a scene without accepting the local light assumption. Once the fallacy of localization has been exposed, any property of an object that has an effect on the character of light at the eye is a potential candidate for the physical correlate of color.

So far we have seen that the local light assumption is false and that it is a special case of a more general fallacy, the fallacy of localization. Now although the local light assumption and its corollary, the illumination dependence of perceived color, are false there is some element of truth to the intuition they express. In some sense it is true that the character of the light reflected from a surface determines the color that a surface is perceived to have. The mistake the local light assumption makes is assuming that it is the character of the light reflected from a surface independently of the light reflected from other surfaces in the field of view that determines perceived color. The character of the light reaching the eye from a given surface will determine the color the surface is perceived to have in a given context of overall retinal stimulation. In order to back up this claim, I will discuss the theory Land has proposed to explain his experimental results. We will see that supplementing the local light assumption with a consideration of context will give us a true claim about the physical determinant of perceived color. This discussion will also show that even the supplemented local light assumption does not fully account for what I think is the most important fact about human color vision, namely, color constancy.

In order to explain Land's theory it will be necessary to provide a few facts about the structure of the human eye. The most important thing to remember is that the human eye contains three classes of what are called cone photoreceptors. There is also a fourth class of photoreceptors called rods but they function chiefly in night vision and make little if any contribution to color vision. Of the three kinds of cones, one kind, the red cones, has its peak sensitivity in the long wavelength region; one kind, the green cones, has its peak sensitivity in the middle wavelengths; and the third, the blue cones, has its peak sensitivity towards the short wavelength end of the visible spectrum. The color terms in the names of these classes should be taken with a grain of salt. They are an artifact from a time when each kind of photoreceptor was thought to produce a characteristic color sensation when stimulated. This theory is false on a number of counts, but notice that if the theory were true the local light assumption would be true and that color constancy would not be possible.

The important fact is that there are three kinds of photoreceptors with differing peak sensitivities. What Land has proposed is that the outputs from each class of photoreceptors are processed independently of the outputs from the other classes. The output from each class of photoreceptors is processed to compute what Land calls lightnesses. Each point in the retinal image is assigned three lightness values, one for each of the three kinds of photoreceptor. It is this triple of lightnesses that, according to Land, determines the perceived color of any point in the visual field.

The lightnesses associated with a given point in the retinal image are computed by comparing the outputs of the photoreceptors at that point with the outputs of the receptors at other points. Take the red cones, for example. The long wavelength lightness for a given point in the retinal image is computed by comparing the output of the red cone associated with that point to the output from the other red cones in the retina. I won't discuss Land's proposed algorithm for this computation, but it can be shown that it is equivalent to comparing the long wavelength intensity at a particular location to the geometric mean of long wavelength intensities at all locations.[6]   The long wavelength lightness associated with a given point in the retinal image is the ratio between the intensity of long wavelength stimulation at that point to the average long wavelength stimulation.   The lightnesses associated with the other wave bands are computed similarly.   The perceived color of a surface, according to Land, can be predicted accurately from knowledge of the triple of lightnesses assigned to that surface.   Experiments done using the techniques described earlier confirm this claim.   Each triple of lightnesses is associated with a unique perceived color.

We now have an explanation of the experimental results described earlier.   It is not the absolute level of flux in each waveband that determines the perceived color of a surface but rather the flux in each waveband relative to the average flux in each waveband.   Surfaces reflecting the same absolute flux in each waveband will not, in general, be perceived to have the same color.   Only if the average flux over the entire visual field is the same will two surfaces reflecting the same absolute levels of light in each waveband appear the same.

We are also now in a position to see exactly how the local light assumption went wrong.   The local light assumption amounts to assuming that it is the absolute flux of light in each waveband that reaches the eye from a surface that determines the perceived color of that surface.   Land has shown that this is not the case.   We can, however, see what is true about the local light assumption.   The character of the light reaching the eye from a surface will determine the perceived color of the surface given the overall character of the light reaching the eye.   Instead of a function from the character of the localized light to perceived color, we have a three-place relation between local light, global light, and perceived color.   The perceived color of a surface depends not just on the character of the light reflected by that surface but also on the character of the light reflected by the other surfaces in the visual field.

We have seen that information about the color of a surface is carried by light in a non-localized form.   If the local light assumption is revised to claim that the perceived color of a surface is correlated with the character of the light reaching the eye from that surface given the character of the light reaching the eye

[6]David H. Brainard and Brian A. Wandell, "An Analysis of the Retinex Theory of Color Vision," *J. Opt. Soc. Am. A* 3 (1986): pp. 1651–1661.

from the other surfaces in the visual field, we have a true claim. This claim by itself does not bring out the most interesting fact about the way in which the color specified by local light is dependent on the global character of the light reaching the eye. The color specified by light of a given character is dependent on the overall stimulation in just such a way as to lead surfaces to have illumination-independent colors. Color constancy is achieved by making perceived color dependent on both local and global properties of light.

Land's theory is one explanation of how color constancy is obtained. Perceived color, in Land's view, is determined by the triple of lightnesses associated with a given surface. This triple of lightnesses will remain the same throughout a wide variety of changes in illumination. To see how this is so consider a fixed scene such as one of Land's Mondrians. Under a given illumination we compute the lightnesses for a given part of the scene by comparing the flux from that area with the average flux for the entire scene. If we change the illumination, then the flux from that part of the scene will change. The flux from all the parts of the scene will change in the same ratio and the ratio between the flux from that area and the average flux over the entire scene will remain the same. The lightnesses associated with a given surface will be the same under a wide variety of illuminations. Land's theory provides an explanation of how color constancy might be achieved.[7]

The failure of the wavelength conception and the facts of color constancy suggest the identification of color with surface spectral reflectance. There are, nevertheless, problems with this proposal. One is that color constancy is not perfect. There are circumstances in

[7]Although Land's theory deals well with the illumination independence of perceived color it is flawed in certain other respects. In computing lightnesses on the basis of the average flux reflected from a scene he makes perceived color dependent on the composition of the scene. For example, the average flux in a scene composed of surfaces of varying shades of red will differ from that of a scene composed of surfaces of varying shades of blue. This difference will remain across changes in illumination and Land's algorithm will predict that a surface viewed in one context will appear a different color from its appearance in the other context. Human color vision is not as sensitive to changes in scene composition as Land's theory implies. In the last chapter I briefly discuss a recent theory of color constancy that supercedes Land's theory in many respects and promises to provide a more satisfactory treatment of these problems. For a discussion of these issues see Brainard and Wandell.

which an object with a fixed reflectance can appear to change in color. This problem can be solved by distinguishing between the physical identity of color and the causal determinant of perceived color. We need to distinguish between real and apparent colors. Colors are identical to reflectances but there are circumstances in which we misperceive color. Theories such as Land's can give us an empirical understanding of how processes that normally allow the recovery of surface reflectance from the light available to the perceiver may fail. A similar account can be given for other properties such as size. Claiming that physical size is the physical correlate of perceived size does not commit us to claiming that we always correctly perceive the size of objects. Similarly, claiming that colors are identical with surface reflectances does not commit us to claiming that all our perceptions of color must be correlated with surface reflectance.

Campbell challenges the legitimacy of any distinction between real and apparent color. According to Campbell:

> The real colour cannot be determined by appealing to standard conditions of observation unless these conditions include a specification of the observer's adaptive state. But then the real colour cannot be accorded any ontological pre-eminence over its rivals. For nothing *in rebus* distinguishes the 'real' red from the 'merely apparent' purple or *vice versa*.[8]

Although Campbell's argument is directed towards the wavelength conception of color, it applies equally well to an identification of color with reflectance. Objectivist theories of color require a distinction between real and apparent color in order to account for those cases in which the perceived color of an object is different from that expected on the basis of its physical constitution. In so far as Campbell's argument blocks attempts to draw such a distinction, it poses a serious obstacle to objectivist theories of color of any kind.

There are two components to Campbell's argument. First he argues that the distinction between what is real and what is merely apparent is drawn for the primary qualities in terms of the interactions of bodies with each other. According to Campbell, we can distinguish between an object that is really six feet long and an object that merely appears to be six feet long because objects that are six feet long have a characteristic pattern of causal effects on other bodies. He then asserts that the distinction cannot be drawn in this way for colors because colors have no characteristic mode of

[8]Campbell, "Colours," p. 146.

interactions. The second part of Campbell's argument consists of an attempt to distinguish real and apparent colors in terms of standard observation conditions. He concludes that no such attempt will succeed because essential elements of the set of observation conditions must be chosen in an essentially arbitrary way. According to Campbell, any distinction between real and apparent color is merely pragmatic and has no ontological significance.

Both components of Campbell's argument are misguided. Colors do have characteristic, if limited, modes of interactions with other bodies. Campbell is right in his claim that the association of particular physical states of affairs with particular experiences is in a sense arbitrary, but wrong in his claim that this fact carries ontological significance. The same claim of arbitrariness can be made against primary-quality perception and the presence or absence of characteristic modes of interaction with other bodies is irrelevant to this charge. The identification of color with reflectance is fully defensible against the arguments made by Campbell.

Campbell is wrong in maintaining that red things have no causal powers in virtue of their redness. More accurately, to assume, as Campbell does, that there are *no* characteristic causal interactions that things have in virtue of their color is to assume the falsity of an objectivist theory of color. Objectivism about color requires that there be some method of determining the color of objects that is independent of the reactions of human perceivers. If there is to be such a method, then there must be characteristic ways colored things have of interacting with the inanimate environment. To bluntly claim, as Campbell does, that objects do not have characteristic causal interactions with their environment in virtue of their color is simply to deny objectivism with respect to color. These interactions need not be very significant and may play little or no role in explanations of the behavior of inanimate objects. If an objectivist account of color is possible differences in color must make some difference in the causal powers of objects.

If color is reflectance, then colored objects will interact with their environment in a specific manner. In this view, an object's color is just an aspect of its characteristic way of interacting with light. Objects of one color reflect light in one manner and objects of another color reflect light in a different manner. The color of an object will not in general affect its interaction with other macroscopic bodies. The color of an object will have no influence on those mechanical and dynamical properties of objects that are most important in explaining the movement and interaction of ordinary objects. It makes no difference to the flight of a golf ball whether it is white or orange. It would be a mistake, however, to assume that the only properties governing the interactions of objects are those that are traditionally supposed to be essential to body. Modern physics attributes many properties to objects, as well as introducing new kinds of objects, that have no obvious influence on the gross behavior of macroscopic objects. To find the characteristic causal powers of colors we must look to subtler effects. Some of the characteristic ways in which colors interact with light are well known. For example, it is common knowledge that black objects placed in the sun will be hotter than white objects. A room with its walls painted yellow will be much lighter than one with walnut paneling. If you hold a dandelion under a friend's chin, their skin will appear to take on a yellowish tinge. These are all examples of causal powers objects have in virtue of their color.

In rebutting Campbell's claim that "Colours have no characteristic modes of interaction,"[9] I do not mean to deny that colors are not basic physical properties. All the characteristic modes of interaction that are possessed by color may have explanations in terms of more fundamental physical properties. We may explain the disposition of an object of a particular color to reflect certain percentages of the incident light in terms of the electronic structure of the atoms that make up that object. This argument is not meant to establish that the omission of color from physics implies a lack of explanatory power on the part of physics. Even derivative and complex physical properties have characteristic modes of interaction with other entities although these interactions may be capable of deeper explanation.

The other component of Campbell's argument against the propriety of a distinction between real and apparent color involves a charge of arbitrariness. Campbell points out that the color an object appears to have depends not just on external circumstances but also on the state of the perceiver. He points out that adaptation phenomena imply that perceived color depends on the recent history of stimulation of the eye and not just on the current stimulus. Exposing an observer to light of a particular character can shift the perceived color of objects subsequently perceived. If an observer in an otherwise dark room fixates a red spot for a few minutes, his eyes will adapt to the particular character of the light reaching them. If he is subsequently exposed to lights that differ in color, his perception of their color will be shifted towards green. The

[9]Ibid., p. 144.

commonly accepted explanation of such phenomena involves differential fatigue of the three receptor systems involved in color perception.

Campbell uses the existence of adaptation to argue that any distinction between real and apparent perception is arbitrary. In discussing attempts to identify the color of an object with the pattern of light at its surface, Campbell argues that:

> There is no clear sense in which the real colour *is* red rather than purple or brown or some other colour no one ever sees. The question 'Which pattern is to be identified with which colour?' has an unambiguous answer only if some adaptive condition in the perceiver is chosen as standard. But to insist that the circumstances leading to one adaptive state enable us to see colour aright, while all others turn vision awry, is to be partial beyond reason. It involves determining the real colour of a surface (which is supposed to be an objective, physical property) on grounds totally remote from the physical circumstances of the surface (*e.g.*, that it looks magenta to normal eyes after exposure to room sunlight, although not otherwise).[10]

Campbell is arguing that any association between color and physical facts is arbitrary because in order to succeed it must assume some special state of the perceiver has been specified, but there are no grounds to support such a specification.

There are two important points to make about Campbell's argument. First, the arbitrariness problem is not solved by the fact that colors have characteristic modes of interaction. Second, the arbitrariness argument applies to primary qualities such as shape or length as well as to colors. The arbitrariness problem is not avoided, as the structure of Campbell's discussion suggests, by an appeal to the characteristic ways bodies have of interacting with each other. Once we have an association between experiences and physical states we can make use of objective criteria to establish whether an object is really red or not. In order to apply these criteria, however, we need to have answered Campbell's question, "Which reflectance is to be identified with which color?" Campbell's point is that there is nothing in the physics of light and reflection that determines that a particular reflectance is to be identified with what we see as one color rather than what we see as another color. The variability of perceived color with adaptive state seems to preclude any non-arbitrary choice of conditions that allows us to perceive the true colors of things.

---

[10]Ibid., pp. 145–146.

This charge of arbitrariness could arise with respect to the perception of shapes and sizes as well as of colors. Our perception of the shape or size of an object can be incorrect just as our perception of its color can be. Berkeley made much of the fact that perception of primary qualities is subject to the same sort of relativity as is secondary-quality perception. Even the analogue of adaptation can arise in the case of perception of shape. If an observer looks at a display consisting of curved lines, after a time the lines look less curved; if the display is replaced by one containing straight lines, the straight lines now look curved in the opposite direction from the curved lines in the original display.[11] This effect is analogous to that seen with color vision. There we have fading of color and displacement of subsequently viewed objects towards the complement of the original color. Since primary-quality perception is subject to the same sorts of illusions and changes as color perception it is also open to the same sort of charge of arbitrariness. We can, it seems, sensibly ask, "Which shaped line is to be identified with which perception of shape?" Since a straight line, depending on the state of the perceiver, can give rise to a perception of either straightness or curvedness any particular choice for associating phenomenal shapes with physical shapes will be arbitrary.

Another and perhaps more familiar way of making Campbell's point is to consider the effects of changes in the perceptual system of human beings. An argument on this basis against the objectivity of color, which he calls the phenol argument, is made by Jonathan Bennett.[12] Bennett's argument attempts to establish that primary-quality perception is not subject to the same sort of arbitrariness as is secondary-quality perception, particularly, color perception. Bennett asks us to consider the effects of certain sorts of changes in the perceptual systems of human beings. In particular, Bennett asks us to imagine that something brings about widespread changes in the color perceptions of human beings: "Mass microsurgery might bring it about that no human could see any difference in color between grass and blood."[13] If this sort of change were

[11]Irvin Rock, *Perceptual Adaptation*, New York: Basic Books, 1966, p. 186.

[12]Bennett, "Substance, Reality, and Primary Qualities," in *Locke and Berkeley*, edited by C. B. Martin and D. M. Armstrong, pp. 105–107. The argument takes its name from the substance phenol-thio-urea which tastes bitter to most people but is tasteless to a significant minority. Bennett uses this substance as an example of the sort of relativity he claims is involved in all secondary quality perception.

[13]Ibid., p. 105.

accomplished, according to Bennett, it "would bring it about that grass was the same color as blood."[14] Change in the perception of humans would thus bring about changes in the colors of things. As we saw earlier, this sort of relativity with respect to color is a common accompaniment of subjectivist views of color. The structure of Bennett's argument is peculiar in that he assumes relativity and uses it to argue for subjectivism.

Bennett's reason for supposing that there is a difference between primary and secondary qualities with respect to this thought experiment lies in the varying difficulty of making sense of the right sort of perceptual change. According to Bennett, we can easily imagine someone who is unable to distinguish red from green but to make sense of someone who was unable to distinguish curved from straight sticks we must also suppose that he suffers a host of other perceptual inabilities. Someone who cannot visually distinguish curved things from straight things must also be unable to tell that when he holds a curved stick next to a straight stick that the ends fail to meet. If such a person were able to see that the ends fail to meet, he would be able to tell there are two kinds of sticks. In general, if we suppose that someone has a defect in the perception of some primary quality, we must suppose that person to have a whole host of related perceptual defects.

The upshot of all this is that Bennett does not find it possible to produce an analog of the phenol argument for the primary qualities. He claims:

> The trouble we meet in trying to reproduce a primary-quality analogue of the phenol argument is that we must either (a) allow the analogy to fail by supposing only that erstwhile spheres "look cubic" in some very restricted sense, e.g., in the sense of presenting visual fields like those now presented by sugar cubes when seen at rest (while in all other ways looking and feeling spherical); or (b) allow the analogy to fail by telling an astronomically complicated story in which not only the shapes of erstwhile spheres but also thousands of other aspects of the world were perceived differently; or (c) insulate shape from its present correlates by means of some radical conceptual revision which has no analogue in the phenol argument.[15]

The phenol argument succeeds for the secondary qualities because their connection with other properties and the behavior of objects are so few. Primary qualities, on the other hand, share so many

[14]Ibid., pp. 105–106
[15]Ibid., pp. 116–117.

connections with other properties that no analog to the phenol argument is possible.

There are two points to be made about this argument of Bennett's. First, colors do have at least some relations among themselves and to other properties. A room with yellow walls will appear to be more brightly lit than a room with blue walls. A person unable to distinguish blue from yellow would still be able to distinguish the different light levels in the two rooms. In order for his perceptual abnormality to be undetectable by him, we must also suppose that he is unable to detect differences in brightness of illumination. This sort of example is not as striking as the ones generated from failures of primary-quality perception, but color is nevertheless connected to other properties.

Similarly, the system of interconnections among primary qualities that Bennett relies on only constrains the sorts of perceptual change that are possible in primary-quality perception and does not outlaw it altogether. Bennett acknowledges as much in part (b) of the passage quoted above although overstates the difficulty in consistently propagating changes in primary-quality perception. For example, we can imagine someone whose ability to distinguish lengths visually is inferior to that of a normal person. To such a person two objects that would look different in length to a normal person would appear the same in length. This possibility is realized by the many people who actually have such a visual defect. If such a person does not compare his experience to that of a normal perceiver, his perceptual abnormality may vary well go undetected. Bennett gives plausibility to his discussion of such examples by supposing gross changes in the ability to distinguish primary qualities. Less drastic changes may very well be undetectable in just the way he claims secondary-quality changes are. Bennett overstates the difficulty in consistently propagating changes in primary-quality perception. The difference in respect of the phenol argument between primary and secondary qualities is one of degree, not of kind.

This brings us to the second point. Given that both colors and the primary qualities are subject to the phenol argument, although to different degrees, the argument cannot carry the ontological weight that Bennett wishes it to carry. In Campbell's vocabulary, the association between perceptual state and physical quality is arbitrary for both primary and secondary qualities. Bennett's discussion establishes that there are more constraints governing the association in the case of primary-quality perception than there are in the case of secondary-quality perception. The existence of this kind of difference between the two sorts of qualities does not imply that one sort is relational while the other sort is not. Although this difference may affect the difficulty of constructing situations in which objects have changed their properties, the difference is one of degree, not kind. We have already seen that the explanatory irrelevance of color is not an obstacle to its objectivity and Bennett's argument amounts to little more than an extended demonstration of this difference between color and size and shape.

It is important to distinguish between two very different ways in which the assignment of properties to objects might be relative to perceptual experience. The arbitrariness of the association between color experience and physical fact implies that if our perceptual systems were different the color experiences we currently have might have had different content. An experience that, given our current constitution, carries the information that an object has one kind of reflectance might instead have carried the information that an object has a different kind of reflectance. We can imagine people who, in looking at a red thing, have the sort of experience we have in looking at green things. Similarly, *pace* Bennett, we can imagine people who, given certain global changes in their perceptions of shape, have the sort of experience we have in looking at a straight line while looking at certain types of curved lines. The sort of relativity assumed by Bennett, however, is very different from this sort of arbitrariness. In Bennett's account, in a world in which the association between color experience and physical fact were different, the colors of things would be different. The phenol argument assumes that if we were all to wake up tomorrow totally color blind then objects would only differ on the black-white dimension, and all the chromatic distinctions that used to be made would have vanished. The physical differences that ground the differences between colors as we currently perceive them would continue to exist but they would no longer amount to differences in color. The main point here is that the first sort of relativity applies equally to primary and secondary qualities, and that there is no reason to suppose that either color or the primary qualities are subject to the second sort of relativity.

Bennett's argument takes as a premise the relativity of colors to color perception. He assumes that a change in the way most people perceive colors would imply a change in the colors of things. Other than his discussion of the explanatory irrelevance of color he gives little argument for this assumption. The sort of relativity assumed by Bennett comes very close to assuming the subjectivity of color. In fact, it is only if subjectivism with respect to color is assumed that a strong case can be made for the relativity of color. The relativity of color in writers other than Bennett is usually seen as a consequence of subjectivism and not as an argument for the mind dependence of color. This argument is not available to Bennett. Bennett cannot both assume the relativity of color and use it to argue for subjectivism and at the same time assume subjectivism and use it to argue for relativity. The relativity of color is not an obvious truth, and we will see in the next chapter that it poses serious problems for subjectivist analyses of color. Bennett's argument from different kinds of misperception only establishes a difference in degree between primary and secondary qualities, not a difference in kind. Primary-quality perception is subject to just the same sort of attack as secondary-quality perception. The only difference between the two is that we have to exercise greater care in proposing changes in the perception of the primary qualities than with color.

5

METAMERS

IN THE LAST three chapters I have considered various arguments against the possibility of objectivist analyses of color and have argued that these arguments leave open the possibility of a particular sort of physicalist analysis. The main alternatives to a physicalist view are various forms of subjectivism with respect to color. Before arguing that my physicalist analysis of color has important advantages over its subjectivist rivals, it is important to distinguish between the two main forms of subjectivism with respect to color and the other secondary qualities.

The first of these views, color phenomenalism, is the antithesis of the physicalism I have been defending. While I have concentrated on colors as properties of objects to the exclusion of colors as characterizing experiences, this view takes the phenomenological aspect of colors as paramount. In this view colors are not properties of external objects at all, but rather of some species of mental object. One person who held such a view is Berkeley. Berkeley, as we saw in the discussion of the argument from microscopes, held the view "that all colors are equally apparent, and that none of those which we perceive are really inherent in any outward object."[1] Or again, "Colors, sounds, tastes, in a word, all those termed 'secondary qualities,' have certainly no existence without the mind."[2] Colors for Berkeley are properties of ideas and not of any external object.

A modern philosopher who holds such a view is Jackson. In his book *Perception*, he argues that colors are properties of mental objects, not physical objects. Jackson claims that "Science forces

[1] Berkeley, *Three Dialogues*, p. 25.
[2] Ibid., p. 28.

us to acknowledge that physical or material things are not coloured . . . . This will enable us to conclude that sense-data are all mental, for they are coloured."[3] The essence of the phenomenalist view is that color is not merely determined by the characteristics of human experience, but is only a property of that experience. The only proper use of color terms in this view is to describe properties of sensations. The ascription of colors to non-mental objects is illegitimate. This view is, on the face of it, highly implausible. The phenomenalist view of colors seems to deny one of the most basic aspects of our common-sense conception of colors. Any view that denies that any external things are colored flies in the face of the way we conceive and talk about colors. In addition, most arguments against a physicalist view of colors that can be drawn from such a phenomenalist analysis of colors can be more plausibly construed as arguments in favor of the second form of subjectivism.

Some writers, such as Locke and Newton, have defended a form of subjectivism that allows the secondary qualities to qualify external objects as well as mental objects. This sort of view, a dispositionalist analysis, has historically been the most important of the varieties of subjectivism and offers the strongest opponent to objectivism about color. Locke, in an often-quoted passage, made the claim that all of the secondary qualities, including colors, "are in truth nothing in the Objects themselves, but Powers to produce various Sensations in us."[4] It is important to realize that Locke is not denying that the secondary qualities are properties of objects. In the dispositional view, colors and the other secondary qualities are properties of external objects. They are the dispositions of those objects to produce certain sensations in us. The intention of denying that colors are anything in the objects themselves is to make the experiences of the perceiver what determines the possession of a particular color. What makes an object red as opposed to green is the sort of sensations it produces in a perceiver rather than any intrinsic property of the object itself.

It is important for the dispositional view that the sensations of the perceiver be definitive of the colors of the things observed by him. If the dispositional view merely asserts that red things have a disposition to cause experiences of red, then there would be no distinction between primary and secondary qualities. Objects that are square are disposed to produce experiences of squareness in many circumstances. What the dispositional thesis asserts is the logical

[3]Jackson, *Perception*, p. 120.
[4]Locke, *Essay*, Bk. II, Chap. 8, § 14.

priority of looking red over being red. Although redness is a property that objects can have, contrary to the phenomenalist view, it is how it looks that determines whether or not an object is red. The crucial role of the appearance in the case of color is in supposed contrast with the case of squareness. Although square things are generally disposed to produce experiences of squareness, an object could conceivably be square without manifesting such a disposition. There is no conceptual connection between squareness and visual experience. The dispositional analysis maintains that there is such a conceptual connection between colors and the particular visual experiences. It is not conceivable that an object that is really red could fail to manifest a disposition to produce experiences of red.

One way to express the main tenet of the dispositional view is that it takes being red to be analyzed in terms of appearing red. It is in this sense that the dispositional view is subjectivist. It does not, however, go so far as to deny that colors are properties of non-mental objects and in this respect stops short of the complete subjectivism of the phenomenalist analysis. The dispositional view can be seen as a compromise between the physicalist analysis I am defending and the phenomenalist analysis. It may seem as if it avoids the major pitfalls of both these views and in this respect forms a synthesis between the two. It does not commit the error of ignoring the fact that colors can be used to characterize experiences as well as objects, but it does not make the mistake of carrying the emphasis on appearances to the extent of denying that external objects themselves are colored. In spite of this initial plausibility, there are reasons to prefer a physicalist analysis over the dispositional view. Any physicalist account of color will have to give some account of the use of colors to characterize experience, but it need not give up the objectivity of colors in order to do so. I will now turn to a set of considerations that, although they may initially seem to favor a dispositional view when examined closely, are more plausibly accounted for in a physicalist view.

Before turning to arguments for and against the physicalist view it will be helpful to define this view more precisely. The present proposal takes colors to be identified with surface spectral reflectances of objects. Each color is taken to be identical with a particular surface spectral reflectance. Each distinct reflectance will be a distinct color. In order for it to be true that a given surface has a given color, the reflectance of that surface must be the one associated with that color. The surface spectral reflectance of a surface is the property of that surface that determines what percentage of each wavelength of light that surface will reflect. It is convenient to represent surface spectral reflectances in terms of a graph of wavelength versus reflectance or percentage of light reflected. Figure 1 gives two representative reflectance curves: one for a green surface, and one for a purple surface. It can be seen from this chart that the green object reflects light most strongly in the middle of the visible spectrum and that the purple object reflects most strongly at the two ends of the spectrum. The proposal under consideration is that each such reflectance curve will be associated with a unique color.

Sample Reflectances

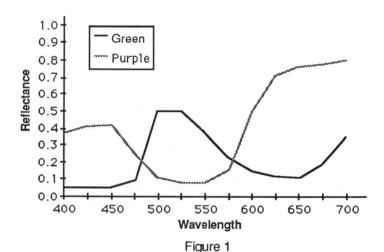

Figure 1

There is a fairly well-known aspect of human color vision that may seem to provide decisive evidence in favor of a dispositional analysis of colors over my physicalist account. The problem is posed by the fact that two physically different surfaces may present the same color appearance to a human observer. That is to say that two surfaces with distinct reflectances may appear to have the same color. In the physicalist account these objects will be different in color in spite of the fact that no normal observer may be able to discriminate them in ordinary lighting conditions. In the dispositional account, on the other hand, the two objects will be the same color in spite of their physical differences: sameness of appearance is sufficient for sameness of color.

The dispositional account seems to give exactly the right account of this phenomenon. It seems absurd to suppose that there are differences of color between objects that are not perceivable by normal human perceivers in normal circumstances. The physicalist account, on the other hand, commits us to supposing that there are differences of color that human beings are not able to detect in normal lighting conditions. Given that there are real physical differences between these objects, the physicalist requires some justification for supposing that these differences are differences in color. Since these differences are not perceived in ordinary circumstances to be differences in color, the burden of argument lies with the defender of the physicalist analysis. If it can be established that there are good grounds for applying the concept of difference in color to these normally imperceptible differences in reflectance, then an important step will have been taken towards establishing the identity of color with reflectance. The existence of imperceptible differences in color would drive a wedge between the characteristics of human color sensations and the attribution of color to objects. If an argument cannot be found for the existence of such imperceptible color distinctions, then the identification of color with spectral reflectance will fail. The task for the remainder of this chapter is to provide the necessary argument.

Two surfaces that are different in their dispositions to reflect light but that are visually indistinguishable are known as metamers. The existence of metamers is a fact about human color vision. They exist for object color perception as well as for the perception of illuminants. Before going on to discuss in greater detail the problems the existence of metamers poses for a physicalist theory of color, it will be helpful to bring forward a few more facts about metamers.

Colors that are metameric for human observers can have very different surface spectral reflectances. Metamerism is not just a matter of objects that differ by imperceptibly small amounts. Some metameric colors differ grossly in the percentages of light that they reflect in different parts of the visible spectrum. Figure 2 shows the spectral reflectance curves for three objects that will appear to have the same color under more or less normal circumstances.[5] As can be seen from the curve, these three objects vary considerably in the large scale way in which they reflect light and not just in the details. Objects with these reflectances will all appear the same shade of gray under some circumstances.

[5]Deane B. Judd and Gunter Wyszecki, *Color in Business, Science, and Industry*, New York: John Wiley & Sons, 1975, p. 158.

The existence of metameric colors is due to fundamental properties of the human visual system. There are only three types of photoreceptors in the human eye that contribute significantly to the perception of color. Any objects that lead to these photoreceptors being stimulated identically in identical viewing conditions will be perceived as having the same color. There are more than three degrees of freedom in surface reflectances, however, so some objects with differing surface reflectances can lead to identical perceptions of color even when viewed under the same illumination and in the same surroundings. In the examples of Figure 2, the same effect is produced on the receptors by an object that reflects all wavelengths equally (1) as by one that has a high reflectance in some parts of the visible spectrum and a low reflectance in others (2,3). In general, there are indefinitely many spectral reflectances that will be metameric with any given color.

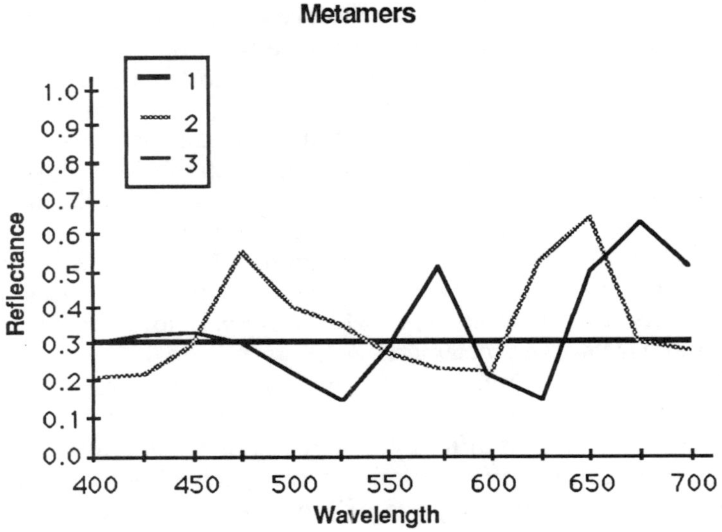

Metamers

Figure 2

Although objects may differ in surface reflectance and still present the same color appearance to a perceiver, any perceived difference in color between two objects will imply that the objects differ in surface spectral reflectance. If two objects are viewed in similar lighting conditions and surroundings and appear to differ in color, then they differ in reflectance. That is to say that, although not every difference in surface reflectance is reflected in a difference in perceived color, differences in perceived color imply a difference in surface reflectance. This point is important in considering the plausibility of the identification of colors with surface reflectances. Although this account implies that some things that look to have the same color are actually of different colors, it does not imply that objects that look different in color can actually be the same in color.[6] In this account, those color distinctions that we do perceive are generally real, but they are not all the color distinctions that there are to be perceived.

It is a general truth that for any two metameric surface reflectances there will be some circumstances of viewing under which the metamerism breaks down. Generally, there will be some illumination under which surfaces with the two reflectances will no longer appear identical in color. If we take the metamers of Figure 2 a monochromatic illuminant with a wavelength of approximately 575 nanometers will bring out the differences in reflectance those objects have at this wavelength. Objects with these three different spectral reflectances will appear to vary in lightness under such an illumination. An observer would perceive three different colors under such an illumination, where under more normal illumination he would have only seen one. This illumination is not the only one that will display the differences in reflectance among surfaces with these three reflectances; depending on the kind of metamerism, there may be many different illuminations that will reveal the physical differences between metameric surfaces to a perceiver. There will always be some lighting condition that will allow an observer to perceive differences between normally metameric colors.

Consider three objects with the surface spectral reflectances given in Figure 2 viewed under an illumination that allows a normal observer to perceive them as different in color. There are two options for a holder of a dispositional view of colors. He can either claim that the objects are now really the colors they are perceived to be under this illumination and consequently different in color, or he can claim that under this illumination the objects merely appear different in color and in fact are all the same color: the color they would appear under more normal circumstances. This second description of the situation involves a sophistication of the dispositional account from the crude form of it described earlier.

---

[6]This statement must be qualified. By using spotlights or differing surrounds objects that have the same reflectance can be made to appear different. These effects involve the creation of color illusions and do not affect the point made in the text.

There are serious objections to accepting either of these options, and no convincing account of such an example is possible given a dispositional analysis of colors.

The first option for the defender of the dispositional view would involve a major revision in our common sense views of the nature of colors. We commonly take colors to be relatively stable properties of objects. In particular, we take the color of an object to be independent of the illumination under which it is viewed. Colors in our common sense ontology are illumination-independent properties of objects. The stability of colors and in particular their illumination independence is reflected in the distinction between real and apparent colors. In the simplest form of the dispositional analysis there is no distinction between real and apparent colors. The apparent color at any given time is the real color of the object at that time. In the example in question, the three objects with differing reflectances are both the same in color and all different in color. There is no conflict involved in this conclusion since on this analysis the objects have changed in color with the change in lighting.

The conflict with common sense views on colors generated by the simple dispositional account has led most defenders of dispositional accounts of color to complicate them by the addition of a distinction between real and apparent color. This distinction is typically drawn in terms of the nature of the perceiver and the conditions in which he is situated. To a first approximation, such accounts will claim that the color of an object is the color it appears to have to a normal perceiver in standard (or normal) conditions. Hume expresses a view of this sort when he claims that "The appearance of objects in daylight, to the eye of a man in health, is denominated by their true and real colour."[7] It is the appearance presented to certain privileged perceivers in certain privileged circumstances that determines the color of an object. The account still takes color appearances as definitive of the colors of objects but it is a restricted class of appearances which determine the colors of objects. In the modified dispositional account, an object is red if and only if it appears red to a normal perceiver under standard conditions. If an object that is red on such a definition appears to be a different color under non-standard conditions—odd lighting, for example—then the perception under the changed conditions is a color illusion. A distinction between real and apparent colors is

[7]David Hume, "Of the Standard of Taste," in *Essays Moral, Political, and Literary*, p. 234.

introduced by restricting the class of appearances that determine the colors of objects.

There are numerous problems involved with spelling out such a modified dispositional view in more detail. For example, it turns out to be remarkably difficult to specify precisely what is meant by 'normal perceiver' and 'standard conditions'.[8] Consideration of examples involving metamers will make my point without considering the details of various dispositional accounts. In order to see the difficulty posed by metamers for the modified dispositional account, I need to fill out my example in some more detail. We need to suppose that the conditions under which the objects with the differing reflectances appear identical in color are those that are identified as standard, whatever they may be. We also need to suppose that the observer to whom the objects appear identical in color meets the criteria for being a normal observer. Whatever the specification of standard conditions and normal observer, it will be possible to identify reflectances that are metameric for those conditions and that observer. If this example is filled out in this way it turns out that our three objects are the same color on this modified version of the dispositional account. When they are viewed under the lighting conditions that reveal their differences in reflectance, at least two of the objects must be appearing to have colors different from those they really have. More importantly, this version of the dispositional account has the consequence that the apparent difference in color displayed by those objects is merely an apparent difference. These viewing conditions produce the illusion that there is a distinction of color where there is none.

In the modified dispositional account there are two sorts of illusions present when viewing the three objects under the monochromatic light. First, there is a color distinction illusion. There appears to be a difference in color between objects that are the same color. Consequently, there is also a hue illusion. Since the objects are the same in color but appear different, at least two of the objects must appear different in color from their actual color. Under the monochromatic illumination of the example, all three will probably appear different from the color they appear in standard conditions, and consequently all three objects will appear different from their actual colors. It is the first sort of illusion, the color distinction illusion, that is important for my argument. The modified

[8]For a discussion of some of the difficulties involved see Clyde Hardin, "Colors, Normal Observers, and Standard Conditions," *J. Phil.* 53, No. 12 (1983): pp. 555–567.

dispositional analysis and my physicalist account differ with respect to the presence or absence of a color distinction in these sorts of cases.

There is an oddity to supposing that when we see the metameric surfaces differing in color we are suffering from an illusion.[9] It is important to remember that there is an objective physical difference among the three objects in the example. Although they appear to have the same color in normal conditions, they do reflect different percentages of light at some wavelengths. It is their dispositions to reflect different percentages of the incident light at certain wavelengths that lead to their appearing differently colored when viewed under some non-standard illuminations. When we see a difference in color between objects with these reflectances under a non-standard illumination, this difference in color is indicative of a real difference in the dispositions of these objects to reflect light. In the dispositional analysis we are committed to saying that we can see a real difference between the dispositions of objects to reflect light by suffering from illusion as to their colors. We can see that the objects are physically different by mistakenly seeing them as different in color. In fact, the only way we can visually determine this physical difference is by suffering from a visual illusion of color difference.

This consequence of the modified dispositional account is very odd. The claim that there are observable physical differences between objects which can only be observed as a result of being wrong about some other property of those objects is highly counterintuitive. The idea that we can get epistemological access to some properties only by misperceiving certain other properties makes the relation between colors and reflectances look very different from what we observe with other perceptual modalities. There are, for example, imperceptible distinctions in physical shape. An account of shape and shape perception that had as a consequence that these distinctions were sometimes observable but only as a result of misperceiving some other property of the object would be highly implausible. This is not to say that the view the dispositionalist is committed to is incoherent, just that it is very puzzling how to make sense of this consequence of it.

Before discussing the implications of this consequence of the dispositional view, I would like to dispose of what might be seen as

[9]My argument here is inspired by Edward Averill's discussion of a similar problem in "Color and the Anthropocentric Problem," *J. Phil.* 82, No. 6 (1985): pp. 281–303.

analogy to the situation the dispositionalist has found himself in. It is quite common nowadays to read of false-color photographs and to get views of celestial objects that are typically with what is called enhanced color. There are other technological devices that allow one to see at night by making temperature differences visible. These various technological marvels might all seem to be ways of seeing that objects have various properties by misperceiving their color. There is a sense in which this is true, but this will not rescue the dispositional analysis from the difficulties it finds in accounting for metamers. It is true that false-color photography represents properties of objects by misrepresenting their colors, but it is not true that we see the object to have colors other than the ones it has. The colors that we see are the colors of the photograph or the video display screen, not of the objects themselves. Inasmuch as these sorts of artifacts usually faithfully reproduce the colors of the objects they represent, the altered forms may induce false color beliefs in those unfamiliar with their special uses. What is important here is that these forms of seeing objects are indirect in a very obvious sense. This indirectness prevents these examples from shedding any light on the position regarding metamers that the dispositionalist is committed to.

We have seen that existence of metamers poses problems for the physical analysis as well as for the dispositional analysis. The physicalist must maintain that objects that appear to be the same color to a normal perceiver in standard circumstances may be different in color. The dispositional view has as a consequence that real differences between objects exist that can only be seen by seeing an illusory color distinction. The physicalist is committed to a much finer grained method of individuating colors than is the dispositionalist. In the physicalist account there are many more colors than human perceivers are capable of discriminating. There is an important insight in the dispositionalist's method of individuating colors, but I will argue that it is applicable to the perception of colors and not to colors themselves. There is something right about subjectivist theories of color and the next chapter shows that in some respects there is less disagreement between the sort of objectivism defended here and the intuitions that underlie subjectivism than there seems. I will first bring forward some more considerations in favor of individuating colors in the fine-grained way that the physicalist is committed to.

A consequence of the dispositional view is a sort of relativism about colors. If we consider perceivers with visual systems that differ from that of a normal human, they may perceive colors differently from the standard observer. Objects that present a particular color appearance to a normal perceiver may present a different color appearance to those with differing perceptual systems. The classical example is that of a perceiver who sees as green what a normal observer will see as red. More importantly in the present context, objects that appear the same color to a normal human in standard circumstances may appear different in color to a perceiver whose perceptual system differs from the human norm. It will, of course, also be the case that objects that appear different in color to the normal observer may appear to be the same in color to such a non-standard observer. This raises the question for the dispositional analysis of what sort of observer is to count as the standard one. The typical response is to relativize color to types of perceivers. Objects are not red *simpliciter* but rather red relative to a certain class of perceivers.[10]

Before considering the consequences of this relativism about color for the dispositional view, it will be helpful to discuss some of the ways in which color perception varies. We can imagine the possibility of a purely phenomenal difference in color perception that has no behavioral consequences. This possibility is the classic example of red-green color reversal.[11] I will not be concerned with

---

[10]A dispositionalist who embraces such a consequence is Colin McGinn. He claims that it "is entirely proper to speak of objects as red with respect to perceiver x and green with respect to perceiver y." McGinn, *The Subjective View*, Oxford: Clarendon Press, p. 10.

[11]It is interesting to note that the actual existence of people with inverted spectra is a consequence of certain views of the mechanisms underlying the most common forms of color blindness. One theory of the origin of color blindness assumes that it is the result of replacement of one or more of the cone pigments by the other cone pigments. This raises the possibility of an observer who, instead of lacking one of the cone pigments, has them swapped. These 'pseudonormal' observers are "characterized by the fact that the R and G cones both contain the 'wrong' pigment. Such an observer would be expected to have normal color vision except that the sensations of red and green would be reversed." Robert M. Boynton, *Human Color Vision*, New York: Holt, Rinehart and Winston, pp. 357–358. It is also interesting to note that there is a striking lack of agreement in the psychological literature about the phenomenal characterization of color blindness of any sort. It seems impossible to come to any conclusion about the character of the color sensations of color blind individuals. Even the study of individuals with one normal eye and one color blind eye has not produced any commonly accepted result. For a discussion of a case of this sort, see Louise L. Sloan and Lorraine Wallach, "A case of unilateral

this sort of change in color perception here. More interesting is the variation in the number and kind of color distinctions that are capable of being made. There are three sorts of variations possible in the ability of a perceiver to see color distinctions. A given perceiver may only be able to see some subset of the color distinctions that a normal human observer can make. The color distinctions such an observer is able to make are the same as ones made by a normal human, but he is not able to perceive all the color distinctions a normal human is able to. Perceivers are also possible that see all the color distinctions that a normal human can and more. The set of color distinctions such an observer can make is a superset of the ones perceivable by a normal human. The first of these sorts of variations is realized by some color-blind people. Depending on the form of the color-blindness, such an observer may agree with the color matches made by a normal observer but will fail to distinguish some colors that a normal observer is able to distinguish. The second of these sorts of variations is less clearly realized by existing perceivers. Some people are better at seeing color distinctions than others but it is not clear whether this is the result of perceptual differences or whether they are merely more attentive observers. The variation is, in any event, much less striking than in the case of color-blind individuals.

The third way in which the ability to see color distinctions can vary from the human norm is by shifting the places in which the distinctions are drawn. An observer exhibiting this form of variation may make as many distinctions as a normal observer but will make them in different places. Some objects that look different to a normal observer will appear the same in color to such a non-standard observer and some objects that appear the same to the normal observer will appear different to the non-standard observer. The set of color distinctions seen by such an observer is at least partially disjoint from those drawn by a normal observer. This third sort of variation can be combined with the first two to produce observers who see either more or less color distinctions from the normal observer but also see different ones. The third sort of variation is the most common among human beings and in conjunction with the first kind of variation accounts for the way in which the color

deuteranopia," *J. Opt. Soc. Am.* 38, No. 6 (1948): pp. 502–509. For a critical discussion of these sorts of studies, see Boynton, *Human Color Vision*, pp. 380–382.

distinctions seen by most non-human perceivers differ from the human norm.[12]

Although relativism with respect to colors may have some plausibility when applied to hypothetical and actual non-human perceivers, it seems very counterintuitive to relativize colors within the class of human perceivers. Color-blind individuals use the language and share the color concepts of normal individuals. As we will see shortly, there is variation even among individuals with more or less normal color vision for whom it would be very implausible to claim that their system of color concepts differs from the norm. A correct account of color-blindness must acknowledge that color-blind individuals fail to discriminate some objects that are, even for them, different in color. Color-blind individuals use the same color predicates as normal individuals and their failures to apply these predicates correctly are real failures and not mere differences in usage. Our intuitions about the colors as seen by non-human observers may be unclear but it is a feature of our common-sense concept of color that colors are not relative to the characteristics of individual perceivers.

Given this limitation on the relativity of colors, the defender of the dispositionalist view must give some specification of the normal observer whose color perceptions are to be the ones in terms of which the colors of objects are specified. If there were no variation in human color perception, then this would be a simple task. We would all be normal observers. There is, however, considerable variation among humans in their abilities to perceive and distinguish colors. Considering only the ability to perceive color distinctions, the definition of a normal observer must at least exclude color-blind individuals. The definition will, of course, have to take a number of other factors into account as well. In particular, the definition cannot be merely in terms of the number of color distinctions an observer is able to perceive in normal conditions. Such a definition would not take into account that there is variation among human beings not merely in the number but in the location of where color distinctions are perceived.

[12]Although most organisms have color vision that is inferior to human color vision there are many that have color vision as good or better. All of the three kinds of variation I have described must be taken into account in describing non–human color vision. See Gerald H. Jacobs, *Comparative Color Vision*, New York: Academic Press, 1981.

It might seem that specification of the standard observer is as much a matter for psychology as for philosophy.[13] For a philosopher the possibility of making such a specification will suffice. Color distinctions have practical as well as theoretical significance. Manufacturers are often interested in making sure that different parts of a product will appear to be the same in color and that products manufactured earlier appear the same in color as those manufactured later. For these and other reasons, color scientists have come up with a mathematical definition of a standard observer. The CIE 1931 standard observer consists of set of color-matching functions.[14] These functions allow a determination of whether or not two differing physical stimuli will produce the same perception of color for an observer whose color perception fits the standard. Such a specification seems to be just the sort of definition the dispositionalist needs. If the dispositionalist adopts the CIE standard observer for his normal observer, then a perfectly precise standard for determining whether two objects are the same in color will result. It seems that not only is it possible to specify precisely the normal observer needed for the dispositional analysis of colors, but that such a specification has already been made. Whether or not the CIE standard turns out to be correct, it at least establishes the possibility of defining what is meant by a normal observer.

Suppose that a dispositionalist adopts a specification of the normal observer such as the CIE standard. Objects that appear the same in color in standard circumstances to an observer who fits the specification will be the same color. Given the considerable variation in human color perception, individuals with one form or another of color-blindness, for example, will not be able to perceive many color differences perceivable by the standard observer. There

---

[13]As Saul Kripke points out, there is a problem here for dispositional views. The dispositionalist claims to be analyzing a pre–existing concept of color so the specification of the standard observer should not involve extensive empirical work. The analysis is supposed to give the meanings of our color terms and consequently should not rely on scientific discoveries. I do not pursue this objection in the text. See Saul Kripke, *Naming and Necessity*, Cambridge, MA: Harvard University Press, 1980, p. 140.

[14]The CIE (Commission Internationale de l'Eclairage = International Commision on Illumination) is an international body concerned with defining standards for colors and illuminations. A discussion of the CIE 1931 standard observer and its supplements can be found in Judd and Wyszecki, *Color*.

will be people who see color differences that the standard observer does not see and there will be people who fail to perceive color differences that the standard observer is able to discriminate. The CIE standard represents, roughly, a median derived from experimental data. Most people's perception of color difference and sameness will lie near those predicted by the CIE standard, but many people's color perceptions will differ at least slightly from the CIE standard. Any such specification of the standard observer will exactly match the actual perceptual discriminations of only some people. The variation in human perceptual abilities precludes a definition of the standard observer that applies to everyone.

The consequences of this variability in human color perception for the dispositional account are of two kinds. Since the perceptions of the standard observer determine which color differences are real and which are not, any person who perceptually discriminates colors differently from the standard observer will suffer from color illusions. The most familiar sort of difference is that found with color-blind individuals. Objects that appear different in color to the standard observer can appear the same in color to someone with color-blindness. In such a case the perception of sameness in color by the color-blind observer is illusory. There is a color-distinction illusion. Two objects that differ in color are perceived to be the same. In the dispositional view there are real differences in color that the color-blind observer is unable to perceive in normal conditions. This account is the one implicit in common-sense talk about colors. The physicalist analysis of colors will also have the same consequence. In both the physicalist and dispositional accounts of color, color-blindness is an inability to perceive some real distinctions of color that are perceivable by a standard observer.

Color-blindness, however, is not the only sort of variation possible in human color vision. People who are not color-blind may still disagree about whether a pair of objects are the same in color or not. For any specification of the standard observer there will be people who are capable of perceiving just as many color-distinctions as the standard observer but who will perceive slightly different ones. A non-standard observer of this sort will not have the obvious disability of the color-blind but will nevertheless perceive some color distinctions differently from the standard observer. Some things that look to be the same in color to the standard observer will appear different in color to some people, and some things that look different in color to the standard observer will appear the same in color to the same people. These differences in which things are perceived to have the same color are generally small but they do exist.

This sort of variability in color perception is very widespread. It is precisely this lack of agreement among actual observers in their judgements of color difference and similarity that motivates the use of a standard like the CIE standard observer. Such a standard gives researchers and manufacturers some agreed-on specification of which stimuli will elicit the same response that they can use for their various purposes. A well-chosen standard of this sort although not accurately describing all or even most normal perceivers will not differ too much from the perceptions of any particular person. The fact remains, however, that precisely which physically different objects are metameric is highly dependent on who is looking at them. Whether two objects form a metameric pair for a given observer is dependent on fairly subtle characteristics of his visual system. The source of much of this variability is in the character of the visual pigments in the eye. The lens of the eye is pigmented and there is a layer of pigment over the central area of the retina. The density of the pigments in both these places varies from one person to another, which can affect which objects appear the same in color without necessarily affecting the acuity of his color vision. There are also other more substantial variations in the ability to perceive color distinctions that appear to be due to differences in the spectral sensitivities of the photo-receptors. These differences need not imply any defect in the ability to distinguish colors.

This sort of variation in the ability to perceive color distinctions has undesirable consequences for the dispositional view. The situation is analogous to that discussed earlier with respect to viewing metameric pairs under non-standard lighting conditions. If a person perceives a color difference between two objects that would look the same to the standard perceiver, then that person is suffering from a color distinction illusion. As in the case of viewing metamers under non-standard illumination, the perceiver in this case is perceiving a real difference between the objects by mistakenly seeing them to be different in color. The objects will have different reflectances but the dispositional view will have the same color. The dispositionalist is forced to the view that people whose color vision is more or less normal may suffer from color-distinction illusions under normal circumstances and that these illusory perceptions may convey information about existing physical differences between the objects being misperceived.

As we saw earlier the dispositional and physicalist accounts of colors were in agreement about the correct description of what color-blind people see. Both accounts take color-blindness to be an inability to perceive some real differences in color. When it comes to considering other sorts of variation in the way people discriminate colors, the two accounts diverge. In the dispositional view colors are to be identified by the perceptions of some standard observer. In light of the fact that there is variability in the sorts of reflectance differences people are able to discriminate, the dispositionalist finds himself committed to the view that in normal circumstances many people may mistakenly perceive objects that are the same in color to be different in color.[15] This is in spite of the fact that such people will be reliably perceiving a difference in reflectance by misperceiving a difference in color.

It is important in this context that the differences in reflectance are always perceived as differences in color. This is true in the case of viewing metameric objects under non-standard illuminations and in the case of the differences in which objects are metameric for perceivers who differ from the standard perceiver. I am not arguing from perceived differences in, for example, texture, to real distinctions in color, but rather for more liberality in the restrictions on whose perceptions and in what circumstances are indicative of a real difference in color. In general, a perceived difference in color implies a real difference in color no matter what the circumstances or the characteristics of the perceiver. On the other hand, perceived sameness of color does not imply real sameness of color at the level of individuation we are now dealing with.

The physicalist account of colors offers a much more natural account of the phenomena surrounding metamers. By identifying individual colors with individual surface spectral reflectances, the account avoids the oddity of the claims implicit in the dispositional account. Instead of contending that differences in reflectance can be perceived by misperceiving differences in color, the physicalist contends that perceiving a difference in reflectance and a difference in color are one and the same thing. By applying the same sort of account the dispositionalist gives of color-blindness to all the phenomena surrounding metamerism, the physicalist achieves a simplicity in his account that is not available to the

[15]It may even be most people. Depending on the precise nature of the variation in color perception among humans it very well could turn out that any specification of the standard observer applied precisely to only a small subset of people. I think this is in fact the case. See Judd and Wyszecki, *Color*.

dispositionalist. There are a large number of possible distinctions in color, only some of which are perceivable by a normal perceiver in normal circumstances, and not all of these distinctions are perceivable by any given perceiver in any given set of circumstances. All possible distinctions of color are perceivable by any perceiver in the right circumstances. By specifying which distinctions are perceptible in which circumstances, we can give descriptions of the variations in non-human color perception as well as the variations in human color perception. At the finest level of discrimination colors are the same for all color perceivers.

I have argued that we should individuate colors in a very fine-grained way. Every difference in reflectance implies a difference in color. One point to make about this identification of colors is that the account of color I have been calling the physicalist analysis is merely an extension of some of the features of our common-sense way of thinking about colors. The physicalist account does less violence to our intuitions about when objects are the same and when they are different in color. There are, however, features of our ordinary conception of colors that are not completely accounted for in the account as it stands. I have said nothing about the use of our ordinary language color terms and very little about the relation between this account of what colors are and how they are perceived to be. I will deal with some of these issues in the next chapter.

The second point is that although colors are individuated in a more fine-grained manner than our perception in ordinary circumstances would allow, not every physical difference in the way objects interact with light implies a difference in color. Reflectances are dispositional properties of objects. The surface spectral reflectance of an object is nothing more than its disposition to reflect different percentages of different wavelengths of light. Objects with the same surface spectral reflectance could differ greatly in the sort of physical mechanism that underlies the disposition. For example, some objects have a reflectance of the type associated with blue things as a result of internal scattering. Short wavelengths are much more strongly backscattered than long wavelengths and the result is a particular kind of reflectance and color. An identical reflectance could be achieved by selective absorption of a long-wave light which is physically a very different sort of mechanism. Even the actual quantum mechanical processes that produce a given absorption can vary from one kind of colored object to another.[16]

There are no grounds for individuating colors in a more fine-grained way than reflectances. At the level of reflectances, we have as many color distinctions as are perceivable. Any difference in reflectance between two objects will be perceivable as a difference in color under some illumination.[17] This will not be true if we move to individuating colors in terms of the physical mechanisms required to produce reflectances. Objects with identical reflectances will never be perceived to have different colors no matter what our choice of illumination. With reflectance we have the limit of what is perceptible with the naked eye. Although I am not tying the concept of color to features of our perceptual experience, there is no reason to suppose that there are differences in color that we are incapable of perceiving under any circumstances.

Although I have been calling my account of what colors are a physicalist account, this may be slightly misleading. If to be a physicalist about colors implies believing that they can be reduced to interactions of the fundamental particles and laws of quantum mechanics, then my analysis of colors is not a physicalist analysis. I do not see how to identify reflectances with any of the fundamental entities of quantum mechanics or any non-disjunctive collection of such entities. In any event, my main purpose is to show that colors are objective properties of external objects and establishing their identity with reflectances satisfies this object.

[16]For a description of the various mechanisms that affect the ability of surfaces to reflect light see, Nassau, *Physics and Chemistry of Color.*

[17]This is not quite right. There are limits to the resolution of human color perception just as there are limits to the resolution of size perception. What is true is that any difference in reflectance that is resolvable will be perceivable under some circumstances. Issues related to the limited resolution of human color vision are the subject of the next chapter.

6

INDETERMINACY AND COLORS

I HAVE JUST argued that there are good reasons to identify colors at the finest level of discrimination with surface spectral reflectances. Each individual color is to be identified with a particular surface spectral reflectance. We also saw, however, that objects with significantly different surface spectral reflectances can in some circumstances appear to be the same color to a human observer. This fact, the existence of metamers, poses an apparent problem for identification of colors with particular reflectances. As a result of the existence of metamers, our perceptions of color do not always allow us to discriminate between objects with different reflectances. I have no account so far as to how it can be that there are colors that are perceptually indiscriminable but physically very different. I need some account of the connection between individual colors, i.e. reflectances, and our perceptions of them. It is simply not true that our perceptions of color stand in a one-to-one correlation with particular reflectances.

Similar problems arise with respect to English color terms. A word such as 'red' is applied to objects with widely varying surface spectral reflectances. Even more specific color terms such as 'scarlet' or 'Oxford blue' are very crude ways of classifying objects in terms of reflectance. Just how crude our color vocabulary is can be seen by considering the fact that the number of perceptually discriminable colors is on the order of ten million. Reference works on color terms include at most a few thousand different color names, but most of us have color vocabularies far smaller than this. When the existence of metamerism is added to this, it can be seen that objects with a large number of different reflectances will have even the most specific color term correctly applied to them. Although I have

101

argued that colors can be identified with reflectances, it now appears that individual reflectances are, at best, tenuously connected with the colors that we see and talk about.

The solution to these problems will have the same form for both color perception and color language. Color terms and color perception are indeterminate with respect to reflectances. Surface spectral reflectances are the maximally determinate colors. Our color language is less determinate than our perceptions of color, but not even our color perceptions correspond to completely determinate colors. When we see that an object is a particular shade of green, we are not necessarily seeing that that object has some particular reflectance, but rather that it has a reflectance that has a particular property or falls into a particular class. Similarly, for an object to be crimson is for it to have a reflectance with a particular form, although with color terms the properties of reflectances they correspond to are more abstract than in the case of perceived colors. What we need to realize in order to avoid these problems is that neither perception nor language are perfectly determinate. In both perception and language we are given kinds of colors, not maximally determinate colors themselves. As we saw in the discussion of the argument from microscopes in Chapter 2, the partial nature of perception is an important component of anthropocentric realism.

The indeterminacy of color perception with respect to the underlying physical facts is not unique to color perception. All perception is indeterminate as well as all measurement. Our perceptions, as well as physical measurements, do not allow us to know, for example, the precise length of an object. Our perceptions of length do place constraints on the range within which the determinate length of the perceived object can lie. This sort of indeterminacy is also familiar to us from measurements of physical quantities which are usually reported with the margin of error attached. Our perceptions of length tell us not that an object is exactly ten inches long, but rather that an object is about ten inches long. For an object to be about ten inches is for it to have length that differs only slightly from ten inches. The exact range of lengths compatible with a particular perception of length will be partly a function of the viewing context, i.e., distance from perceiver, orientation, and lighting, and partly a function of the characteristics of the visual system of the perceiver. The perception of color does not differ in this respect from the perception of length. Objects whose reflectances differ very slightly will be indistinguishable. There will be a range of reflectances compatible with any given color perception.

The existence of metamers shows, however, that colors are indeterminate in a way that differs from lack of precision in estimates of length. Metamers do not differ just slightly in their reflectance profiles. An object with an essentially flat reflectance curve can appear to have the same color as one with large peaks in its reflectance. The sort of imprecision involved here is apparently very different from the sort involved in ordinary measurement. The situation with respect to colors seems analogous to supposing that a four-inch stick could look the same as one that was either two or six inches but not the same as one that is three inches in length. An even better analogy is with shape perception. It seems bizarre to imagine that a rectangle might be indistinguishable from a hexagon but not from a pentagon. Yet this seems to be exactly the situation with respect to the perception of colors. An object which reflects equally in all areas of the visible spectrum can be indistinguishable from an object that reflects very strongly in some areas and very weakly in others.

The nature of the indeterminacy of color perception is a consequence of the characteristics of the human visual system. In order to understand this indeterminacy and see that it is not essentially different in kind from the indeterminacy involved in primary-quality perception, it will be helpful to look fairly closely at the problem the visual system faces in trying to determine the colors of the objects within its field of view. If we abstract the problem of determining the reflectance of an object from the limitations of the human perceptual system (or any other physically realizable device), we discover that there are essentially two different strategies that might be pursued for measuring reflectances: an active and a passive approach. The active approach involves differentially illuminating the the object of interest while the passive approach involves making use of the existing illumination. Both approaches have to deal with the fact that the reflectance of a surface can, in principle if not in fact, vary arbitrarily with wavelength. In order to specify completely the spectral reflectance of a surface, we must be able to determine the percentage of the visible light the surface reflects at each wavelength throughout the visible spectrum. The two approaches differ in how they approach the problem of determining the reflectance of a surface at a very large number of different wavelengths.

The standard approach to measuring the surface spectral reflectance of an object in the laboratory is a version of the active approach. This technique makes use of a device known as a recording spectrophotometer.[1] A typical recording spectrophotometer contains a single photocell which is capable of reporting the total energy incident on it from the entire visible spectrum. It also contains a light source or sources which are capable of providing monochromatic (single-wavelength) illumination throughout the visible spectrum. The reflectance of an object is determined by illuminating it with light of a single wavelength and recording the output of the photocell for that illumination. If we repeat this process for each wavelength in the visible spectrum, we have a record of the amount of light the object reflects at each wavelength. If we know the energy of the illuminant for each wavelength, then we can determine the surface spectral reflectance of the object by simple division of the recorded values by the illuminant values.[2] There are two important points to notice about this method of determining surface spectral reflectance: (1) it requires complete control over the illumination of the object of interest, and (2) it requires only a single kind of photoreceptor to measure surface spectral reflectance throughout the visible spectrum.

Passive methods of measuring surface spectral reflectances do not require control over the illumination of the object of interest. They attempt to measure the reflectances of objects by using properties of the light reflected from objects under whatever illumination they happen to be found. The leading examples of passive systems, of course, are the various forms of color vision utilized by living things. There are two problems facing a passive method of measuring reflectance. First, there must be some method of measuring the energy of the light reflected from an object at each wavelength in the visible spectrum. This problem is solved by the active method by illuminating the object with a series of monochromatic lights. Second, the contribution of the surface spectral reflectance of the object being measured to the light reaching the measuring instrument must be separated from the contribution of the spectral power distribution of the light illuminating the object. This problem is the problem of how to achieve color constancy which was the focus

---

[1]Judd and Wyszecki, *Color in Business, Science and Industry*, pp. 91–102.

[2]In practice, it turns out to be very difficult to calibrate light sources accurately enough to perform this procedure. Most recording spectrophotometers contain a reference sample whose surface spectral reflectance is known and the amounts of light reflected from the test object at each wavelength are compared to the amounts reflected from the standard rather than with the amount emitted by the illuminant.

of discussion in earlier chapters.[3]   In this chapter I will assume that the respective contributions of the illuminant and surface reflectance have been successfully disentangled and focus on the problem of how the spectral power distribution of the light reflected from an object is measured.   It is the way in which the human visual system solves this problem that is the source of the indeterminacy in human color vision.

The most obvious way of measuring the intensity of the light reflected from an object at a large number of different wavelengths would be to have a different sensor type for every wavelength of interest.   This can be accomplished either by having receptors that are sensitive to only a single wavelength or by having a single type of receptor and some system for separating the light by wavelength before it reaches the receptors.   In either case, the resolution of the system depends on the number of different receptors the system possesses.   To accurately measure the surface spectral reflectance of an object would require a very large number of receptors.   An additional requirement for accuracy in a passive system for measuring reflectance is that the illumination of the object being measured covers the entire visible spectrum.   If there are wavelengths which do not occur in the illumination, then there is no information in the light reflected from the object about the object's reflectance at those wavelengths.   We are all familiar with an extreme example of violation of this constraint: colors cannot be seen in the dark.

There is one important similarity between these two different approaches to measuring reflectance that is not a feature of human color perception.   Both approaches to measuring surface spectral reflectance display only the sort of indeterminacy that we are familiar with from other kinds of physical measurement. It will not be possible to make perfectly accurate measurements with either system.   There are two sorts of effects that combine to generate this indeterminacy. First, the sensors involved will have some error associated with them. The value of the reflectance for a particular wavelength will have a degree of imprecision.   In addition, active systems cannot illuminate objects with every wavelength in the visible spectrum, nor can passive systems have a

[3]Land's theory, discussed in Chapter 4, provides one account of how color constancy might be achieved by the perceptual system.   In the next chapter I will discuss the work of Maloney and Wandell, which provides a more explicit account of how to separate the effects of surface reflectance and illumination. See Maloney, *Computational Approaches to Color Constancy*, and Maloney and Wandell, "Color constancy: a method for recovering surface spectral reflectance."

sensor type for every wavelength in the spectrum. The spectrum is continuous and physical devices must be finite. These facts imply that objects whose reflectances differ only at closely spaced wavelengths will be indiscriminable. These two effects combine and consequently the measurements of such a system will be indeterminate with respect to the determinate surface spectral reflectances they are measuring. This indeterminacy will be exactly similar to the sort of indeterminacy of other measuring devices such as scales or micrometers. Any measurement made by such devices is compatible with the actual value falling within a small range surrounding the measured value. In the case of our reflectance measuring instruments there will be a margin of error for the reflectance at each wavelength. Any reflectance that falls within this margin of error at each wavelength will result in the same measured value. Although measuring instruments cannot provide us with the maximally determinate values of the quantities we are attempting to measure, they can provide us with perfectly objective information about indeterminates under the same determinable.

It is important to emphasize that the indeterminacy of measurement does not impair the objectivity of measurement. In spite of the fact that any particular measurement of length, for example, is compatible with the measured object's having any of a range of lengths, the measurement still provides perfectly objective information about the length of the object. There may be no interesting physical property of the object taken by itself that corresponds to having a length in a certain range. The degree of indeterminacy of a measurement is determined by the measuring instrument, and not by the object itself. None of this impairs either the objectivity of the measurement nor its ability to convey useful information about the length of an object. The only important fact is that whether or not an object has the property of having its length within a certain range depends solely on the determinate length of the object. As long as this is true, the object will have any given indeterminate length independent of the existence of any perceiver or measuring instrument. Although the imprecision of measurements of length is more familiar than the imprecision of measurements of reflectance, the cases are exactly analogous. Indeterminacy does not impair objectivity.

Perception, of course, differs in many important respects from measurement with physical instruments, but it does not escape from the lack of precision that is inescapably a part of all measurement. Our primary-quality perceptions are subject to error in this sense just as much as are the determinations of measuring devices. We should not, however, be misled by the use of the term error to describe this sort of lack of precision in perception and measurement. It is not that measurements and perceptions misrepresent the qualities that they purport to give information about. They merely fail to specify completely the quality in question. Although my perception of the length of an object may be compatible with the object having any of a range of different lengths, my perception is not misleading as to the length of the object. It simply does not tell me all there is to know about the length of the object. Once again, we need to be careful in our analysis of the relation between perception and reality in order to avoid the fallacy of total information.

We have already noticed that color perception exhibits the same sort of indeterminacy as does length perception. Two objects whose reflectances are very similar may look to be the same color to a human observer. We also noted that color perception exhibits a form of indeterminacy that seems very different from the sort of indeterminacy one finds in the perception or measurement of length. Metameric objects can have reflectances that are very different from one another. We cannot claim, as we can in the case of length perception, that our perceptions of color tell us that the peaks in the reflectance and their heights fall within a certain specified range. The relation between perceived color and reflectance is much more complicated than the relation between perceived length and length. Our discussion of primary-quality perception in conjunction with our discussion of the varieties of reflectance measuring systems, however, has given us the tools we will need to understand the source of this complexity and the essential similarity between color and length perception.

If we consider color perception in light of the distinction between active and passive reflectance measuring systems, it is clear that human color vision is a passive system. Human color vision typically takes place under broad-band illuminants that are under at most crude control by the perceiver. We make use of existing illumination in order to perceive the colors of the objects around us. Since human color vision is a passive system, its precision is limited, as we have seen, by the number of types of sensors available to it. If reflectances are allowed to vary arbitrarily, complete specification of the surface spectral reflectance of any object will require a sensor type for every wavelength in the visible spectrum. That attaining this kind of accuracy is not feasible for the human visual system was first recognized almost two hundred years ago by Thomas Young. Young argued:

As it is almost impossible to conceive each sensitive point of the retina to contain an infinite number of particles, each capable of vibrating in perfect unison with every possible undulation, it becomes necessary to suppose the number limited, for instance, to the three principal colours, red, yellow, and blue . . . and that each of the particles is capable of being put in motion less or more forcible, by undulations differing less or more from a perfect unison . . . and each sensitive filament of the nerve may consist of three portions, one for each principal colour.[4]

Although Young misidentified the three primaries, he got the number of sensor types operative in human color vision exactly right. Human color vision involves three types of receptors, each of which has its own characteristic sensitivity. The sensors responsible for human color vision are all sensitive to a broad range of wavelengths and their ranges of sensitivity overlap considerably. These receptors are sensitive only to the total amount of light they receive in the range of wavelengths to which they are sensitive. They do not give any information about the distribution of energy within their range of sensitivity. As a consequence, any pair of objects that reflect the same amount of light within each of the three wavebands will produce the same response from the sensors.

We now have an explanation of the occurrence of metamers. Metamers are objects with surface spectral reflectances that, although different, reflect the same amount of light within each of three wavebands corresponding to the sensitivity ranges of the human photoreceptors. The visual system is unable to distinguish metamers because the information in the light that specifies their differences is not available to it. The limited number of sensors possessed by the human visual system limits its abilities to fully determine the reflectances of the objects in the visual field. The complexity of the indeterminacy involved in color vision is a result of the visual system's having to make do with only three receptor classes in attempting to specify the reflectance throughout the visible spectrum.

Not only do we now have an explanation of the mechanisms that result in the existence of metamers, it is even possible to speculate as to the reasons for having such a small number of receptors. There are practical pressures to keep the number of receptors small with both organisms and machines. Since receptors occupy space, the number of different wavelength-selective receptor types in a receptor array influences the spatial resolution of the receptor

[4]Thomas Young, "On the theory of light and colours," in Herrnstein and Boring, pp. 13–14.

array. Assuming constant receptor size, if each point in the field of view of a receptor array is sampled by four different types of wavelength-selective receptors, lower spatial resolution will be possible than if fewer different types of receptors were used. There is a tradeoff between spatial resolution and wavelength resolution in constructing any sort of visual sensing system. Given the relatively greater importance of spatial information over color information for most purposes, it seems likely that most visual systems will have relatively few receptor types in the interests of maximizing spatial resolution. More speculatively, there is also evidence to suggest that in most situations relatively few receptor types are sufficient to specify exactly the reflectance of the objects in a given scene. Naturally occurring illuminations and reflectances do not vary arbitrarily, and it may be possible to correctly identify the reflectance of naturally occurring objects using as few as four, and possibly three, receptor types.[5] Although given the tradeoff between spatial resolution and color resolution some degree of indeterminacy may be unavoidable, the indeterminacy in practice may not be as great as theory would suggest for either organisms or artificial vision systems.

In spite of the complexity of the constraints color vision places on reflectances, there is nothing essentially different from the sort of indeterminacy one finds in other sorts of measurement or perception. The perceived color of an object constrains the values its surface spectral reflectance may have, just as the perceived length of an object constrains the values its length may have. The only difference is in the form of the constraints, not in the fact of indeterminacy. Just as in the case of length, instruments for measuring surface spectral reflectance may display exactly the same sort of indeterminacy as human color vision. Any passive system with the same number of sensor types will display the same kind of indeterminacy as does human color vision. The fact that the relation between perceived color and determinate color is more complex than the relation between perceived length and determinate length is no argument that the one quality is more subjective than the other. In both cases, one can give a description of the class of determinate properties that is consistent with any given perception that makes no reference to subjective characteristics of the

---

[5]Maloney, *Color Constancy*. In fact the restriction to naturally occurring objects is not necessary. Technology has only succeeded in complicating the situation with respect to illuminants and not with respect to object reflectances.

percept. Although the classes that our perceptions of color sort reflectances into are determined by the peculiar characteristics of our color vision apparatus, it is possible to specify these classes in a perfectly objective manner.

This last claim may be the subject of some dispute. Most philosophers have supposed that if precise specification of the categories into which our color perceptions sort physical objects is possible at all, it must be done disjunctively.[6] As the existence of metamers establishes, there is no physically interesting property shared by all and only those things that appear to be any particular shade of color. This has led philosophers to suppose that the only description one can give of the information about the physical world obtained in any given color perception must be of the form 'The object has property F or property G or property H . . .' We might think that the only description possible of the range of reflectances compatible with a given color perception would have to be of the form 'Has spectral reflectance F or has spectral reflectance G . . .' Such a description would be very complicated and would contain a very large number of disjuncts if it would be possible to state it all. If this situation did in fact obtain, it would make the sort of indeterminacy involved in color perception look very different from the sort of indeterminacy involved with the perception of other qualities such as length or shape.

There is reason to believe, however, that we can do much better in specifying the nature of the indeterminacy inherent in color perception than this disjunctive view would indicate. Again, the analogy with length perception is instructive. It might seem that the set of lengths compatible with a given length perception is similarly complicated. There is no interesting physical property shared by objects whose lengths are 10.1", 10.2", 9.9", and 9.8", although they all may appear to be the same length. If we had to construct a disjunction in these terms of all the determinate lengths compatible with a given length perception, it would be very long and possibly infinite. If we consider, however, what it is that the various determinate lengths have in common from the point of view of the visual system, we discover that there is a simple mathematical expression that allows us to specify the range of lengths compatible with a given length perception. Objects whose difference in length is less than a certain limit will appear to be

[6]Smart, *Philosophy and Scientific Realism*; Shoemaker, "Review of Colin McGinn: *The Subjective View*," *J. Phil.* 83, No. 7 (1986): pp. 407–413; Campbell, "Colours."

the same length. Thus although there is no physical property tying together all objects that appear to have a particular length there is an objectively specifiable, albeit anthropocentric, property that such objects share.

In the case of color, it is possible to give a simple mathematical description of the range of reflectances compatible with a given color perception. Without going into all the technical details it is possible to say a few things about this property.[7] The basic insight is that human color vision is what I have termed a passive system with three types of broad-band sensors. As we have seen, objects that reflect the same amounts of light in each of the three wavebands will appear to have the same color.[8] We can express the common property that the reflectances of such objects will share by summing the reflectances of the objects over each of three ranges. We will obtain what is called a triple of integrated reflectances.[9] Each member of this triplet expresses the reflectance of the object summed over one of the bands of wavelengths corresponding to the sensitivity of one kind of photoreceptor. Triplets of integrated reflectances defined in this way prove to be very well correlated with perceived color.[10] Objects that share the same triple of integrated reflectances will appear to have the same color in most circumstances and objects that differ significantly in their triple of integrated reflectances will appear to differ in color. Triples of integrated reflectances appear to play the same role in color perception that ranges of lengths do in length perception. Although somewhat more complicated to specify, the nature of the indeterminacy involved in color perception is not ultimately different in

[7]For a discussion of this subject, see Land, "The retinex theory of color vision."

[8]This claim is not true in all circumstances. As a result of the mechanisms underlying color constancy, even objects that reflect identical amounts of light at each wavelength in the visible spectrum can appear to have different colors. What is true is that in a given context of viewing objects that affect the sensors identically will appear the same color and this is all I need for my present purposes.

[9]I have omitted a scaling factor that represents the variation in sensitivity of the receptors with wavelength. This scaling merely serves to make the color space defined by the triples have spacing closer to the perceptually determined spacing. See Land, "The retinex theory of color vision."

[10]McCann, McKee, and Taylor, "Quantitative studies in retinex theory: A comparison between theoretical predictions and observer responses to the 'Color Mondrian' experiments," *Vision Res.* 16 (1976), pp. 445–458.

kind from that involved in the perception of primary qualities such as length.

Earlier I made use of the fact that perceptions of difference in color generally implied difference in reflectance while perceptions of color identity did not generally establish identity of reflectance. We are now in a position to understand why there is this asymmetry between perceptions of color sameness and difference and to see that the perception of other qualities shares this asymmetry. This asymmetry is a simply a consequence of an aspect of the indeterminacy of perception that has not been emphasized so far. If two objects appear to have the same color, then in the account of color perception I have offered they will both fall under the same color indeterminate. Falling under the same color indeterminate, however, is no guarantee that they will be the same fully determinate color. As we have seen, color perception involves a substantial amount of indeterminacy, and surfaces with quite different colors can fall under the same perceptual indeterminate. Objects that have the same color appearance need not be identical in color. The same situation arises with respect to primary-quality perception. Two objects that present the same length appearance need not have the same determinate length. This is just what is meant by the claim that perception is indeterminate.

The fact that perceptions of difference are generally true of determinate qualities and not just of perceptual indeterminates is a consequence of the fact that perceptual indeterminates are in general mutually exclusive. In most circumstances two objects with the same reflectance will appear to have the same color. There will, of course, be exceptions to this rule. If we are clever with the lighting in the scene or in the arrangement of differently colored objects in a scene, we can make two surfaces with the same reflectance appear very different in color. Similarly, we can arrange conditions so that two lines with the same length appear to have different lengths. The Müller-Lyer illusion shown in Figure 1 is an outstanding example of a situation of this sort. Situations involving illusion aside, however, perceptual indeterminates are in general mutually exclusive. Perception is in general a *function* of the perceptual situation and as a consequence each distinct determinate property is associated in a given context with exactly one perceptual indeterminate.[11] It is the indeterminateness of perception in combination

[11]There are exceptions to this generalization. Cases of ambiguous stimuli are the subject of much discussion in the psychological literature. Reversible figures such as the Neckar cube provide

with the mutual exclusiveness of perceptual indeterminates that accounts for the asymmetry between perceptions of sameness and difference. This is just as true of visual perception of primary qualities as it is of color perception.

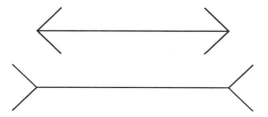

Figure 1. Müller-Lyer Illusion

It should be apparent that the relation between perception and reality is the same in color perception as it is in primary quality perception. The puzzling phenomena of color vision all find their analogs in the perception of primary qualities. We have seen that perception of primary qualities such as length or shape is indeterminate. The indeterminacy of color (reflectance) should come as no surprise. We have also seen that the indeterminacy displayed by perception is also a feature of instruments used to measure the qualities that we perceive. This is just as true in the case of color as it is for any of the primary qualities. In perception we do not gain knowledge of determinate properties, but only of whether the determinate qualities of objects fall in certain ranges. The main difference between the perception of length and the perception of color is in the nature of the constraints that perception places on the determinate properties of the objects perceived. In the case of color these relations between perceptual indeterminate and determinate properties are much more complicated than they are in the case of a primary quality such as length. This difference in the type of indeterminacy is not, however, a sufficient reason for supposing that the identification of color with reflectance is inconsistent with the nature of our experience of color.

---

examples of this sort of stimulus. The existence of such examples do not refute the point made in the text that perceptions of difference are more generally accurate than perceptions of sameness.

The identification of colors with reflectances raises similar problems in both perception and semantics. Both the words we use to talk about color and our perceptions of color are color indeterminates. Color terms are very crude, even in terms of our color experience. A term like 'red' covers a wide range of reflectances and is correctly applied to objects that produce a wide range of color experiences. One way to see how crudely our color language classifies the world is by looking at a book of color samples. An example is the *Dictionary of Color* by Maerz and Paul.[12] This book contains 7056 color samples and contains a list of 4000 color names. Although the color vocabulary of Maerz and Paul is extraordinarily large (as befits the authors of a dictionary of color), many of their samples have no names associated with them. The number of perceptually discriminable colors is at least two orders of magnitude larger than the number of samples in Maerz and Paul, which gives some idea of how crudely our language classifies colors.

Our perception of color has an anthropocentric character, and our color language is, not surprisingly, hopelessly anthropocentric in the way it classifies objects by color. The broadest color terms vary widely in how much of color space is included in their extension. Blue, for example, extends over a wide range of lightness and saturation. Sky blue and navy blue are both equally blues. Red, on the other hand, although covering a wide range of lightnesses, is only applied to colors that are fairly saturated. Desaturated reds are not reds at all but pinks. Yellow is applied over a wide range of saturation but only to very light colors. Dark yellows are not even really yellowish, but are rather a sort of greenish brown, or olive. Terms for various shades of color vary widely in their degree of specificity. Sky blue refers to a small family of desaturated and light blues, while some terms such as viridian are even more specific. Not every group of perceptually similar colors receives a name. There is no apparent pattern to which groups receive names and which do not, nor is there any apparent order to the inclusiveness of those color names that are assigned. Color terms are also language relative. For example, there are words in Russian for light blue and dark blue but no word that includes all the things

[12]A. Maerz and M. Rea Paul, *A Dictionary of Color*, New York: McGraw-Hill, 1950. Another, more comprehensive, list of color names can be found in Kenneth L. Kelly and Deane B. Judd, *The ISCC–NBS Method of Designating Colors and A Dictionary of Color Names*, National Bureau of Standards, 1955.

that an English speaker would call blue.[13] This situation is of course exactly what should be expected. Our color language reflects not only the peculiarities of the human visual system but also our interests and the nature of the environment we find ourselves in. It would be very strange if our common use of color language did not reflect these various factors.

In spite of this highly human-centered aspect to our color terms, I will argue that color language is no more subjective than our perception of color. Color terms refer to kinds of reflectances. For an object to be red in my account is for it to have a reflectance that falls within a particular class. Whether or not a particular color term is correctly applied to some object depends only on whether or not that object's reflectance falls within the class referred to by that term. These classes will, in general, be highly anthropocentric. We saw in our examination of color perception that being anthropocentric was no obstacle to objectivity and the same is true of our use of color language. The extensions of most color terms will look bizarre and arbitrary from the viewpoint of the physicist, but this merely displays that their interest lies elsewhere. As long as we can specify the reference of color terms without making use of subjective facts, their objectivity will be unimpaired, no matter how unnatural the kinds they pick out may be.

It is an important feature in this account of colors that it is capable of reproducing at least some of the common-sense truths about colors. An analysis of color in which it is not true that orange is more similar to red than it is to blue seems not to be an analysis of *color* at all. Although, as we will see, there is some dispute as to which truths about colors are central to our concept of color, at least some pre-analytic statements about color must come out true in any serious account of color. An important feature of our concept of color is that colors are relatively stable, objective properties of material things. My analysis of colors clearly preserves this feature. Another feature of colors which I have not emphasized but which also is clearly compatible with my account is that colors are all (in)determinates under the same determinable. Colors are all kinds of reflectances. The different degrees of preciseness in color specification correspond to different degrees of determinateness in the specification of reflectances. What may not be so obvious is

[13]A survey of the variation in color terms across a large number of languages can be found in Brent Berlin and Paul Kay, *Basic Color Terms: Their Universality and Evolution*, Berkeley, CA: University of California Press, 1969.

that this account of the nature of color and colors preserves many of the less abstract characteristics of common-sense thought about colors.

Colors have a variety of similarity relations. It seems an indisputable truth that orange and red are more similar to each other than either is to blue. Other clear truths about colors include statements such as "Brown is darker than yellow" or "Scarlet is a shade of red." The connection of these truths with the kinds of reflectances referred to by the color terms that occur in them is not obvious. There is no immediately clear sense in which one kind of reflectance is darker than another, and it is at least disputable that the kinds of reflectances associated with various color names actually stand in the relationships that we commonly suppose that the colors do. It is, in fact, possible to account for many of these truths but in doing so it will be important to keep in mind the anthropocentric nature of our color language.

In order to make it plausible that this analysis of color can account for the sorts of statements mentioned above, it will be necessary to look briefly at the kind of reflectance associated with a color term such as 'red'. The relativity of our color language to the characteristics of our perceptual system becomes obvious when we look at the class of reflectances that fall under a color term such as 'red'. One might think that it might be possible to specify the class of reflectances that red things have by a description such as 'a surface spectral reflectance is part of the reference of red if and only if it is high in the long wavelength portion of the spectrum and low elsewhere'. Although a more precise version of this sort of description may pick out reflectances that only red things have, it will not pick out all the reflectances that an object can have and still be red. The problem with this sort of description is the one we are familiar with from our consideration of metamers. It is the total amount of light in the sensitivity range of each kind of receptor that is important for color perception and not how the light is distributed within these ranges. An object can have its highest reflectance in the middle of the visible spectrum, the region usually associated with perceptions of greenness, and still look red. Unless we have some reason for excluding these sorts of cases we cannot give a description of this sort for the reference of our color terms.

Our earlier discussion of metamers, fortunately, provides the tools needed to solve this problem. Triples of integrated reflectances provided a way of classifying reflectances that corresponded to the discriminatory abilities of human perceivers. They also provide a way of expressing the similarity relations that we wish to capture. Just as in the case of perception, triples of integrated reflectances provide the needed bridge between determinate surface spectral reflectances and the properties of interest to human beings. If we think of triples of integrated reflectances as coordinates in a three-dimensional space, then similar colors will occupy adjacent regions of that space. I will call the space defined in this way *color space*.[14] Every reflectance will have a location in this space. There will be a volume of color space which contains the triples of integrated reflectances associated with red things and an area of color space which contains the triples of integrated reflectances associated with blue things. The correct description of the reference of red will be of the form, 'a surface spectral reflectance is part of the reference of red if and only if the triple of integrated reflectances associated with it occupies region R', where the specification of region R is in terms of the space of triples of integrated reflectances.

We are now in a position to see that many truths about color are preserved by this analysis. Statements about the relations between colors and their shades are easily expressible in terms of kinds of reflectances. One color is a shade of another color if and only if the kind of reflectance associated with the second color is included in the kind of reflectance associated with the first. 'Scarlet is a shade of red' will be true just in case all the reflectances in the extension of 'scarlet' are included in the extension of 'red'. There will be some borderline cases in which it is not clear that the reference of the narrower term is completely included in the reference of the broader term. For example, it may be true that 'Blue-green is a shade of green', although there are examples of blue-green which are not clearly green. Such cases, if they exist, are due to the fuzziness of the borders of color categories and not to problems with the inclusion criterion. I will not deal with the possibility that at the boundaries of color categories there may be no clear answer as to whether or not something is a member of that category. Fuzziness of this sort would raise no special problems for my theory, so I will in general assume that the boundaries of color categories are perfectly precise.

Statements about similarity between different colors can also be given a simple analysis in terms of kinds of reflectances. A state-

[14]This idea is developed in Land, "The retinex theory of color vision"; and Land, "Recent advances in retinex theory and some implications for cortical computations: Color vision and the natural image."

ment such as 'Orange is more similar to red than it is to blue' will be true if and only if the location in color space of the class of reflectances referred to by 'orange' is closer to the location of the class referred to by 'red' than it is to the location of the class referred to by 'blue'. Since color space is constructed to mimic the way in which the human visual system classifies reflectances, perceptual similarity will in general correspond to contiguity in color space. Two colors that look very similar will be located very close to each other in color space, and colors that look very dissimilar will be widely separated. The interpretation of statements of color similarity and dissimilarity is straightforward in terms of statements about relative location in color space.

Color space will also help to us to understand what the reference of judgements of brightness and darkness are in my analysis. Generally, objects that reflect more light will be brighter than objects that reflect less light. In terms of color space, distance from the origin will be correlated with the brightness of a particular color.[15] The further from the origin a triple of integrated reflectances is located, the more light is reflected by objects with that integrated reflectance. A statement that brown is a dark color will be true if the reference of brown in color space is located close to the origin. Judgements of relative brightness will be interpreted in terms of comparative distance from the origin of color space. The general strategy of how truths about colors are to be fitted into my account should now be clear. Relations between colors are seen to be relations between locations in color space. Color space is specified completely objectively, so the various color relations have an objective basis. Color space is also structured in the same way as our perceptual color judgements so that there can be no conflict between true perceptual judgements and the objective facts. The reference of color terms and the relations and properties they instantiate are objective although anthropocentric.

[15]The scaling factor mentioned in note 8 is especially important when considering the brightness of colors. The visual system is much more sensitive to some wavelengths of light than it is to others. Failure to include this factor would mean that colors that are equally distant from the origin could have very different brightnesses.

7

THE REALITY OF COLOR

THE MAIN OBSTACLES to an objectivist theory of color have now been overcome, so long as we retain a clear understanding of what is essential to objectivity. We can be color realists so long as we are anthropocentric realists. I have argued that the objectivity of color does not depend on its use in scientific explanations and that objectivity is consistent with arbitrariness and anthropocentrism. All that is necessary for the objectivity of a property is that objects have or fail to have that property independently of their interactions with perceiving subjects. Color is objective in so far as the colors of objects do not depend on how they appear to observers, or even whether or not there are any observers. Since we can specify the colors of objects in terms that make no appeal to the experiences of human beings, color is an objective property. The nature of our perceptual experience determines which color categories we perceive but these categories are themselves independent of our perceptual experience. One test for objectivity is the possibility of constructing a device that is capable of determining whether or not objects possess the property in question. If it is possible to build such a device, then we have a demonstration of the fact that properties of human experience do not determine whether or not an object possesses the property.

My defense of the objectivity of color rests on the identification of color with surface spectral reflectance. Color, in this account, is the disposition objects have to reflect varying percentages of the incident light. Surface spectral reflectance is clearly an objective property. The spectral reflectance of a surface is a property that surface has in complete independence of how it appears to any observer or even the existence of any observers. It is possible, as

119

shown in Chapter 6, to construct devices that measure the surface spectral reflectance of an object. Although reflectance is an objective property in this sense and is physically well understood, it is not reducible to more fundamental physical properties. Fundamentally different physical mechanisms can result in objects that possess very similar dispositions to reflect light. The reflectance of an object is a multiply grounded dispositional property. It is not possible to identify reflectances and therefore colors with the possession of any particular physical microstructure. In this respect, my account of color differs from those of other objectivists who suppose that color must be identified with some aspect of the microstructure of objects if its objectivism is to be successfully defended.

The identification of color with surface spectral reflectance explains some of the features of color that have seemed difficult to reconcile with an objectivist account of color. The causal irrelevance of color described in Chapter 1 can now be understood, as well as the fact that this lack of causal power is consistent with the objectivity of color. Reflectance is not among the fundamental properties physical scientists use in explaining phenomena. Instead it is a dispositional property which, although not identical with any particular physical constitution, is well understood in terms of the fundamental properties of physics. In addition, the only causal effects an object has by virtue of its having a particular reflectance are those due to the nature of the light reflected by the object on a given occasion. Since subtle variations in the character of light are typically of little importance in the gross behavior of objects, the fact that colors are of little importance in understanding the behavior of macroscopic objects no longer presents a puzzle. The only familiar results of the color of an object are ones clearly associated with the way in which objects reflect light. Dark objects become warmer in sunlight than light objects because they reflect less of the light striking them than do light objects. The effect of the color of the decor on light levels in a room has a similar explanation. All these effects, including less familiar microscopic effects due to light, will also have, at least in principle, an explanation in more fundamental terms. Although reflectance is a perfectly respectable property which physicists and others have found useful in characterizing objects, it is of limited importance in understanding the causal interactions among inanimate things, especially in comparison to its importance in human experience.

The analysis of color in terms of reflectance also clarifies the nature of another difference between color and properties such as shape or size. Shape and size are perceivable by more than one sense while color is only perceivable by vision. To make this precise we would need to have an analysis of directly versus indirectly perceivable properties, since it is sometimes possible to infer the color of an object from the perception of it via a sense other than vision—taste, for example. Nevertheless there is an association between color and vision that is not typically found with the primary qualities, particularly the spatial ones. This sort of association between vision and color is just what one would expect given the identification of color with reflectance. The color of an object is nothing more than its particular way of interacting with light. The only sense which is sensitive to properties of light is vision, so there is no mystery in the fact that it is only by seeing, as opposed to touching or smelling, objects that we can determine their color. The spatial properties of objects, on the other hand, typically affect the interactions of objects in ways that go beyond their ability to reflect light. The shape of an object is relevant not only to the light it reflects but also to its ability to resist pressure. Consequently, shape is perceivable via both the haptic and visual senses.

In light of the apparent marginality of color in the physical scheme of things, it may appear puzzling why color is such an important property in the biological realm. Color vision is not limited to human beings, and it appears that among the vertebrates the only species completely lacking color vision are a few of the strictly nocturnal ones.[1] Color vision is distributed among all the major groups of vertebrates, and several species of fish and birds appear to possess color vision as good or better than human color vision. Insects are also reported to have color vision, as we would expect, given knowledge of the devices flowers use to attract them for pollination. There is also evidence that some species display color constancy of the kind familiar from studies of human psychology. The perception of color, it seems, must have some utility since the only higher organisms that lack sensitivity to color are those whose nocturnal lifestyles make the perception of color very difficult.

Color, although rarely a cause, is often an effect and as such can serve as an indicator of the presence of other properties. The obvious example to cite is the frequent correlation between color and edibility and taste. It is interesting to note that, in addition to making an association between particular colors and ripeness in

---

[1] Jacobs, *Comparative Color Vision.*

various fruits and vegetables, cookbooks often make reference to color changes in their recipes. These range from the familiar browning of meats to the change in the color of beaten egg yolks that signals when to add butter during the preparation of Hollandaise sauce.[2] In addition to their function as signs of the presence of other properties colors also aid in the identification and re-identification of objects. The reflectance of an object is in general a stable property of objects and as such the possession of a particular reflectance can help in reidentifying particular objects. This process is aided by the fact that naturally occurring objects are very rarely exactly alike in color. In using colors to identify objects, we are able to make use of subtle differences in the surface composition of objects that would be otherwise unavailable. In spite of the limited causal powers of colors, color perception is clearly not a useless artifact of the constitution of the visual system.

Chapter 2 argued that color does not obey the dissectivity principle and consequently that the argument from microscopes fails to establish that there is a conflict between the color a thing appears from a distance and the color it appears from closer up. This argument was primarily conceptual in nature and did not rely on any positive account of the nature of color. With the identification of color with reflectance, we are now in a position to appreciate the failure of dissectivity for colors and to offer a positive account of the relation between the color of an object and the color of its parts. The key to this account lies in the fact that there is often spatial variation in the reflectance of a surface. The reflectance of a surface will typically vary from point to point on that surface, and this implies that if we measure the reflectance of the surface with differing spatial resolution, we will get differing measured reflectances. Spatial variations in reflectance that are smaller than the smallest area that the device is able to discriminate will not be detectable. The reflectance measured by the device for an area at the limit of its resolution will be the average reflectance of that area. If the limits of resolution of the device change, then the averages will be taken over larger and smaller areas. If the reflectance of the object is not uniform, averaging over areas of different sizes can lead to different measured reflectances. Different information about the spatial structure of the reflectance

[2]According to Craig Claiborne, in preparing Sauce Hollandaise one should beat the eggs "until they are thick and pale in color." Claiborne, *The New York Times Menu Cookbook*, New York: Harper & Row, 1966, p. 485.

of a surface will be obtained depending on the spatial resolution of the device doing the measuring.

The relativity of measured reflectance to spatial resolution suggests that the phenomena on which the argument from microscopes relies should be treated in a manner analogous to that given to metamers. The existence of metamers was taken as establishing the limited wavelength resolution of the human visual system and as implying that vision only provides information about kinds of colors and not about fully determinate colors themselves. Similarly the argument from microscopes shows that our perception of color is spatially indeterminate and that it only provides limited information about the spatial distribution of color on objects. Instead of the kinds of color that were introduced in order to account for metamers, it is the average color of an area that is the relevant perceptual indeterminate. This analysis avoids the fallacy of total information by assuming that from any given point of view we only get partial information about the actual distribution of color on a surface. Armstrong and Berkeley erred in assuming that color perception must contain total information about the spatial distribution of color.

Although the phenomena of the argument from microscopes are subject to a treatment analogous to that given metamers, the phenomena themselves are very different. It is important that the reflectance associated with a given area is a fully determinate property of that area. It is the distribution of reflectances, and not the reflectances themselves, that is at issue in the argument from microscopes. If one measures the ratio of the incident light to the reflected light over the entire area, one will be able to determine the reflectance associated with that area with as much precision as the measuring device allows. The indeterminacy enters in the loss of information about the spatial distribution of reflectance within that area, not in the determination of reflectance for the area itself. Another difference from the treatment of wavelength indeterminacy is that the spatial resolution of the visual system is not fixed. One can change the size of the smallest area of a surface one is able to discriminate by changing one's distance from that surface. There is no possibility of changing the wavelength resolution of the visual system. One can also use optical aids to increase the spatial resolution of the eye in a way that is not available for wavelength resolution. It is this ability to change the size of the smallest discriminable area that is responsible for the changes in color appearances from which the argument from microscopes takes its inspiration.

Thus there is no inconsistency between the color of a drop of blood seen with the naked eye and the color of the same drop viewed through a microscope. The size of the smallest discriminable areas are different in the two cases. Consequently, we obtain different information about the color of the object in the two cases. With the naked eye an observer is able to see the color of the drop at a certain scale, and at that resolution the drop is uniformly red. The finer spatial variation in the reflectance of the drop is invisible at this scale. With the microscope we are able to discern the finer details of the spatial variation in reflectance. We can see the reflectance of smaller areas of the drop than we can with the naked eye. Using a microscope, however, it is impossible to *see* the color of the drop at the coarser resolution, although it may be possible to infer the color from the details that are visible. The difference between the two views is in the difference between the sizes of the minimum discriminable areas. Similar remarks apply to viewing objects at different distances without the use of optical aids. The size of the minimum resolvable area of a surface changes with viewing distance and with this change comes the possibility of discovering different aspects of the spatial distribution of color over that surface.

The part/whole distinction of Chapter 2 is also capable of explication in terms of reflectances. The part/whole terminology itself is not always natural when applied to failures of dissectivity. When a plaid shirt is seen from so far away that the pattern is indiscernible, it is misleading to call the color it looks to have from that perspective the color of the whole shirt. In other cases, such as the drop of blood, it is perfectly appropriate to speak of the color of the whole drop. Both cases, however, are given the same sort of analysis in my account and neither raises a problem for the identification of color with reflectance. An examination of Berkeley's example of the drop of blood will help clarify both what we commonly mean by the color of the whole and how the same analysis of the failure of dissectivity for colors can apply to both sorts of cases.

When we look at the drop of blood with the naked eye, there is a minimum discriminable area. The color of the drop from this point of view is simply the colors of these minimum visible areas laid side by side. When we look at the drop through a microscope, there is a much smaller, minimum, visible area. The color of the drop from this point of view is similarly the spatial composite of these minimum visible areas. The areas seen through the microscope are parts of the areas seen with the naked eye. We have seen, however, that the reflectance of a part of an area need not be the same as the reflectance of the whole. Colors are not dissective. What is also true in the case of the drop of blood is that the reflectance of the whole drop is the same as the reflectance of the minimum visible areas as seen by the naked eye. In this sense, it is perfectly accurate to talk of the color of the drop as a whole and identify it with the color seen by the naked eye. If we do not resort to optical aids such as microscopes, the color of the drop will not appear to change. The reflectance of the drop is homogeneous above a very small resolution.

In other cases, such as the example of the plaid shirt, this way of describing how different views of an object are consistent can be misleading. Some objects have large-scale heterogeneities in their reflectance in addition to microscopic ones. Although the same account of the colors of their various parts will apply, it will be misleading to talk of the color of the whole. Our ordinary concept of the color of a whole object only applies to objects which exhibit no changes in reflectance throughout the range of resolutions obtained at normal viewing distances. The color of the whole in ordinary usage is used to describe the color of objects at the range of resolutions obtained under ordinary viewing conditions. In cases such as the drop of blood, anything other than a microscopic view will produce the same determination of reflectance. In other cases, getting very far away may produce a change in color. In all these cases what is true is that different viewing distances can allow us to see different aspects of the color of an object. We can maintain the veridical nature of the colors seen from different viewing distances without supposing that one and the same area can be multiply colored. The part/whole distinction of the earlier chapter applies to areas and their components rather than to objects as we commonly individuate them.

In Chapter 3, I discussed an argument of Aune's that attempts to establish that there is a conceptual conflict between common sense and physics in the attribution of colors to external objects. The identification of color with reflectance evades the force of Aune's argument. We saw that Aune's argument required a modified form of the dissectivity principle to the effect that every part of a material surface must be colored. According to Aune, however, the particles that physicists tell us are the fundamental constituents of the surface are not colored. This leads to an apparent conflict between our common-sense concept of a material surface and the description of the world found in physics.

Some of the fundamental particles of physics are indeed colorless. They do not interact with visible light at all. Other particles interact with visible light when they are organized into systems of certain types. For example, the absorption and re-emission of light by electrons that are part of atoms forms the basis for most of the phenomena of reflection and absorption. Isolated electrons behave very differently from ones bound into atoms, and their particular behavior is very sensitive to the precise nature of the atomic and molecular units in which the electrons occur. It is only when we arrive at the atomic and molecular levels of organization that the phenomenon of selective reflection and absorption of visible light arises. Isolated particles, in general, have no disposition to interact with light in the range of wavelengths to which the human eye is sensitive and consequently are not colored on my account. The identification of color with reflectance gives us an empirical understanding of the failure of dissectivity for color. We now have an understanding not just of the inconclusiveness of Aune's argument, but also an appreciation of the grounds on which its main premise can be seen to be false.

The main concern of the rest of Chapter 3 was the wavelength conception of color and its implications for the objectivity of color. In the wavelength conception, color is to be analyzed in terms of the spectral power distribution of the light reflected by colored objects. An object is a particular color if it is reflecting light of a particular spectral power distribution. This conception of color, as the argument from wavelengths establishes, is not satisfied by colors as they are perceived. There is little correlation in ordinary circumstances between the spectral power distribution of the light reaching the eye from a particular area and the perceived color of that area. If the wavelength conception of color were accurate, then there were would be no possibility of defending a physicalist analysis of color.

Chapter 4 argues that the wavelength conception is flawed. There is no reason to limit the search for the physical basis of color to properties of light, and in particular there is no reason to exclude reflectance from consideration as the physical description of the nature of color. The only argument for the wavelength conception that is available rests on the fallacy of localization. This argument makes the assumption that information about the color of an area must be carried in the light reaching the eye from that area independently of the light reaching the eye from other areas of the field of view. Land's experiments and theory of color vision show both that the wavelength conception is flawed and that, by taking into account the global character of the light reaching the eye, we can compute illumination-independent color descriptors.

Land's experiments are quite striking, and his theory accounts for many aspects of color constancy quite well. There have been recent advances in theoretical analyses of the problems involved in color vision that supersede Land's work in some respects. These advances, if anything, make the identification of color with reflectance even more plausible. In particular, Land's theory does not account for the degree of success the visual system has in determining spectral reflectance and does not provide an analysis of the environmental conditions under which reflectance can be successfully determined. This recent work, by Maloney and Wandell, also provides some insight into the reasons for the failure of color information to be localized in the light reflected from particular areas.[3] Maloney and Wandell approach the problem of color constancy by assuming that the function of color vision is the determination of the spectral reflectance of the objects in the visual field. They investigate the conditions under which the accurate determination of spectral reflectance is possible.

The problem of determining reflectance is underdescribed. We saw in Chapter 6 that there are various methods of measuring spectral reflectance and that they have different conditions under which they can be successfully utilized. Maloney and Wandell analyze the problem as it exists for a generalized model of color vision and under the conditions in which normal color vision takes place. The problem they analyze is that of recovering surface spectral reflectance given only a sample of the light reflected from the surfaces in the field of view and without independent knowledge of the spectral power distribution of the ambient light. They further assume that the reflected light is sampled by a finite number of broad-band photoreceptors, as it is in the human visual system. A full account of their work is beyond the scope of this work but some of their results are interesting and relevant to the issues discussed in Chapters 3 and 4, in particular, the fallacy of localization.[4]

---

[3]Maloney, *Computational Approaches to Color Constancy*, and Maloney and Wandell, "Color constancy: a method for recovering surface spectral reflectance."

[4]The theory of color constancy developed by Maloney and Wandell is very sophisticated and highly technical. In what follows, I present a highly simplified account of those aspects of their theory that are relevant to the issues I have treated in earlier chapters. I do not give

As we saw earlier, the spectral power distribution of light reflected from a surface depends both on the spectral power distribution of the ambient light and the spectral reflectance of that surface. It is this fact that poses the main problem for any attempt to recover the reflectance of a surface from the light it reflects on any given occasion. If only the properties of the light reflected from a single surface of uniform reflectance are considered, then there is no possibility of determining the reflectance of that surface.[5] The necessary information is not present. If we limit consideration to local properties of light, then the problem is insoluble. Maloney and Wandell show that if there are a number of surfaces with different reflectances present in the field of view, then it will sometimes be possible to recover the reflectance of each surface from the light the surfaces are reflecting. They investigate the conditions that must be met in order to allow the measurement of surface spectral reflectance, and they propose an algorithm for doing so.

If reflectances are allowed to vary arbitrarily, then there will be no solution to the problem of color constancy for any system with any finite number of photoreceptor types. Even assuming the illumination is fixed, the problem is insoluble. If the illumination is allowed to vary arbitrarily, then the problem is insoluble in a different way. The number of surfaces of distinct reflectance that must be present in the scene is related to the amount of variation allowed in the light. With increase in the complexity of the variation allowed in the illumination, the number of surfaces of distinct reflectance that must be present in the scene increases. Neither the spectral reflectances nor the lights encountered in nature vary arbitrarily, however, and this is the key to Maloney and Wandell's analysis. If it is possible to model the reflectances and lights that occur in a given environment using models that have only a small number of parameters, then it may be possible to solve the problem of color constancy for that environment. In fact, it appears that the complexity of the variations in reflectance and lighting that are actually encountered are capable of being modeled using a very

anything like a full description of the theory, nor do I make any attempt to reproduce the mathematics involved.

[5]A completely homogeneous visual field produces a constant visual experience that is independent of the particular characteristics of the display. No matter how bright or what color the display would appear if viewed in conjunction with other surfaces it will appear as a grey film. Such a homogeneous field is known as a *Ganzfeld*.

small number of parameters. It is this fact that enables the human visual system to determine reflectance as accurately as it does.

The most important result of Maloney and Wandell's work is that there is an algorithm that operating only on the light reflected from a scene recovers the spectral reflectances of the surfaces in a scene. The identification of color with reflectance does not present the color vision system with an impossible task. Under certain conditions it is, in fact, possible to visually obtain information regarding the reflectances of the surfaces in a scene. The two most important conditions that must be met are that the number of parameters in the model of reflectances must be smaller than the number of types of photoreceptor and that the number of parameters in the model of lights must be less than or equal to the number of surfaces of distinct reflectance in the scene. This second condition illustrates the importance of not assuming that the visual system responds to the light reflected from each area of a scene independently. Color constancy would be impossible if the visual system behaved in this way. If consideration of the light reflected by several areas of the scene is allowed, then not only is color constancy possible but the reflectance of each of them can be determined.

The importance of avoiding the fallacy of localization is only one of the philosophical implications of the work of Maloney and Wandell. As we will see shortly, their theory sheds light on both metamerism and the degree of indeterminacy involved in human color perception. The success of a theory such as theirs also supports the identification of color with reflectance. Their work applies an algorithm designed to recover information about reflectance from light to the explanation of features of the psychology of human color vision. In so far as it is successful, it provides evidence for the view that when we learn the color of a thing we have learned something about its reflectance. If it was not possible to connect human color vision and reflectance in this way, the identification of color with reflectance, would be very implausible. Although the success of theories such as the one under discussion help answer some philosophical questions about the identification of color with reflectance their work by no means implies that an objectivist account such as mine is correct. Objections such as the resemblance thesis of Locke cannot be answered by empirical research. All empirical research can do is provide the appropriate data on correlations between perception and objective fact and establish that the proposed identification of color with reflectance does not make color perceptually inaccessible.

One of the problems posed for a physicalist account of color by empirical research in color vision is accounting for the existence of metamerism. Metameric objects are objects that have different reflectances but appear to have the same color. The existence of metamers implies that there are color distinctions that are undetectable by a normal observer in normal conditions. Although this implication may seem an undesirable one, in Chapter 5 I present an argument that not only makes the existence of color differences that are normally undetectable plausible but presents difficulties for any account of color that denies the existence of such color differences. Metamerism poses a problem for dispositional accounts of color because for any pair of metameric objects there will be some lighting conditions under which they appear to differ in color. This fact commits the most plausible form of dispositionalism to the claim that there are observable physical differences between objects which can only be observed as a result of suffering from an illusion of color difference. A dispositionalist must hold the position that the only way of getting perceptual access to some differences in reflectance is by misperceiving the color of objects having those reflectances. Although this position is not incoherent, it seems epistemologically more acceptable to suppose that some color differences are not perceivable by a normal observer in normal circumstances.

The theory proposed by Maloney and Wandell has interesting consequences for the understanding of metamerism. The existence of metamerism implies that the three photoreceptor types of the human visual system are not enough to accurately determine all the parameters necessary to model naturally occurring reflectances. In order for three photoreceptor types to suffice for the accurate determination of spectral reflectance there can be at most two parameters in the model of reflectance. Although it appears that more parameters than this are necessary, it is not many more. Maloney concludes that a model with as few as three to six independent parameters would suffice to account for most of the variation in surface spectral reflectance.[6] The small number of parameters required to account for existing variations in reflectance implies that metamerism may not be that common. The visual system is not faced with the problem of determining a property that can vary in an unconstrained manner. Although there are possible differences of color that are undetectable in normal circumstances, the actual occurrence of such differences appears to

[6]Maloney, *Color Constancy*, p. 60.

be relatively rare.   In general, objects that look to have the same color will have the same color.

Maloney's analysis has implications for the problems discussed in Chapter 6 as well.   That chapter contains an account of the nature of color perception and language that acknowledges the anthropocentric nature of our perceptual and linguistic color categories but defends their objective nature.   The key to that discussion is the realization that perception and language deal primarily with kinds of reflectances and not individual reflectances themselves.   Our perception and speech are indeterminate in important respects and the nature of the indeterminacy derives in part from the nature of our perceptual system.   In spite of this anthropocentric component to our color categories, the categories, once fixed, are perfectly objective.   Although the nature of our experience helps determine the boundaries of the categories once the categories have been specified, their existence is independent of perceptual experience.   What Maloney's analysis suggests is that these categories may be less arbitrary in physical terms than might have been expected. In spite of the limitations of the human visual system, it may not suffer from a substantial degree of indeterminacy.   Although this does not directly affect my conclusion regarding the objectivity of our perceptual classifications, it is in a sense reassuring to find that the information obtained via color vision places substantial constraints on the reflectances objects can have.   In addition to suggesting that human color vision is reasonably precise in its determination of reflectance, the work of Maloney and Wandell also supports my claim that it is possible to construct a measuring device that could determine which perceptual color category a given object would fall into.   The algorithm for determination of surface spectral reflectance that Maloney and Wandell propose has been used to construct artificial vision systems that determine reflectance under the same constraints that human color vision operates.[7]   These systems classify objects by reflectance in a way that is similar to that of human perception.

No amount of simplification in the kinds of reflectances in the environment will significantly affect the indeterminacy of our color language. Common color terms are very far from naming even individual perceptually discriminable colors, let alone individual reflectances.   The connection of our speech with the reflectances of

[7]Wandell, "The Synthesis and Analysis of Color Images," Ames Research Center: NASA Technical Memorandum 86844, 1985.

the objects to which color words apply is very crude. Just as with perception, however, the degree of indeterminacy in the relation between color words and reflectances does not conflict with the objectivity of the classifications. The beginning of an account of color language is the realization that although our experience plays a role in determining the boundaries of the categories named by color words, once these boundaries are fixed the categories themselves are perfectly objective. Not even perceptual considerations are enough, however, to account for the reference of the color terms we use. The existence of a term for a particular kind of reflectance has at least as much to do with pragmatic considerations as it does with perceptual ones. The existence of languages that divide color space differently from English, even with regard to the most basic color terms, establishes the influence of non-perceptual considerations on our use of color language.

The identification of color with reflectance seems to commit me to a controversial stand on at least two issues not yet discussed in any detail. The first and most important is the nature of color sensation. My account of color clearly precludes color terms having primary and literal application to color sensations. Sensations cannot literally be said to be colored just as in subjectivist views objects cannot literally be said to be colored. Color is primarily an attribute of objects and any attribution of color to sensations or experiences will be in terms of the color of objects. Given this constraint, however, I am not committed to any particular theory of the nature of color sensation. A view such as the intentional object view of Mackie's described earlier is perfectly consistent with my account of the nature of color. There are certainly other possibilities as well. I am also not committed to the reduction of color sensations to brain states or their identification with functional states or any other analysis of the nature of sensation. The identification of color with reflectance settles a metaphysical question about the nature of color but is not tied to the answers to other metaphysical questions having to do with the nature of mind. Although it is impossible to give a satisfactory account of color without some consideration of issues in the philosophy of perception and epistemology, the basic question this account has tried to answer is metaphysical. Broader issues have been included only in so far as they are relevant to answering the metaphysical question that is my main focus.

Another issue that I have ignored until now is how to apply my account to the color of light sources. Light sources do not get their apparent color from their dispositions to reflect light. Although light emitters may reflect light as well as emit it, the reflected light is generally of little importance in determining their perceived color. The difference between a red and green stoplight is not due to a difference in reflectance between the two lights. If this account of color is not modified, we cannot describe the difference between the two lights as a difference in color. They could have identical reflectances and still appear to differ in color.

It is important to note that I am not proposing an account of the color of light beams. In this respect Newton was exactly right: "The rays are not coloured." Newton arrived at this conclusion, however, by way of a subjectivist analysis of color. The point here is simply that light rays are invisible. Although we see by means of light we never see light itself. The colors of light emitters are seen as properties of the emitting surface itself and not as the color of the light it is emitting. Putative counter examples to this position are usually based on a confusion between seeing a beam of light and seeing the dust particles that it is illuminating. Although it is possible to see the path of a laser beam by seeing the particles illuminated by the beam, it is not possible to see the beam itself. If there were no particles to reflect the light of the beam, it would not be possible to see its path. Color is primarily a property of surfaces, and in giving an account of the color of light sources I am giving an account of the color of the emitting surfaces, and not of the light itself.

It is, of course, possible to extend the concept of reflectance and apply it to light emitters.[8] Even in the case of light emitters it is still possible to compute a ratio between the illumination and the light leaving a surface. For ordinary objects this ratio will merely describe the reflectance of the surface, while for light emitters this ratio will take into account the light emitted by the surface as well as the light it is reflecting. A light source will have some component of its spectral reflectance exceed unity, which will distinguish it from surfaces that only reflect the incident light.   The identification of color with this extension of spectral reflectance will make no difference to the account given of object color. It merely provides a way of extending the account to illuminant color.

There is a problem with extending a reflectance-based account of color to light sources in this way. For an object that is not a source of

---

[8]The extension of reflectance to include light emitters is adopted from a similar proposal by Richard Grandy. Grandy, "Red, white, and blue? Stars and stripes? A modern inquiry into the physical reality of colors."

light, its reflectance is a stable, illumination-independent property of that object. Reflectance as extended to apply to light-emitting surfaces will generally vary with illumination. Most light sources emit a fixed amount and kind of light independent of the levels of ambient light. The ratio between the illumination and the light leaving the surface will change as the illumination changes, since the light emitted remains constant. This implies that the color of light sources changes with changing illumination. In this respect there will be a fundamental difference between the colors of objects that merely reflect light and those that are light emitters.

This sort of relativity fits in well with the apparent colors of light sources. We are all familiar with the changes in the apparent colors of light sources with changes in illumination. The flame on a gas stove can appear a brilliant blue when viewed under an incandescent lamp, and nearly invisible in daylight. This suggests that this extension of my account to light sources is on the right track. Since object colors account for the vast majority of color phenomena that we are confronted with, I can be satisfied with having given a convincing defense of the objectivity of object color.

The identification of color with reflectance allows for a coherent account of most of the phenomena associated with color. Philosophical arguments that try to establish the subjectivity of color are either flawed or misinformed. The only serious rival to the physicalist theory of color would be a view of the sort put forward by Newton. Newton's theory of color combines an account of the physical facts underlying color perception with a dispositional account of color itself. The theory of color perception that Newton put forward is flawed, however, as our discussion of the argument from wavelengths established. The dispositional component of Newton's analysis, while consistent with the empirical facts, must also be rejected. The relativity of color to observers that is a consequence of this theory has undesirable consequences of which the most important is the treatment of metamers. An objectivist theory of color can be successfully defended if careful attention is paid to the relevant empirical facts and some account is given of the anthropocentric nature of color perception and language. The compatibility of objectivism with an anthropocentric account of color terms and the categories given in color perception allow the analysis to succeed. Any sensible objectivism must allow that human language and perception provide a characteristically human window into the world. By taking this anthropocentrism into account, it is possible to provide a realist analysis of color that also preserves most of our ordinary knowledge about color.

BIBLIOGRAPHY

Armstrong, D. M. *The Nature of Mind and Other Essays.* Ithaca, New York: Cornell University Press, 1981.

Armstrong, D. M. *Perception and the Physical World.* New York: Routledge & Kegan Paul, 1961.

Armstrong, D. M. *A Materialist Theory of the Mind.* New York: Humanities Press, 1968.

Armstrong, D. M. "Colour Realism and the Argument from Microscopes," in *The Nature of Mind and Other Essays,* 1980, pp. 104–118.

Aune, Bruce. *Knowledge, Mind, and Nature.* New York: Random House, 1967.

Averill, Edward Wilson. "The Primary–Secondary Quality Distinction," *Phil. Rev.* 91 (1982): 343–361.

Averill, Edward Wilson. "Review of *The Subjective View* by Colin McGinn," *Phil. Rev.* 94 (1985): 296–299.

Averill, Edward Wilson. "Color and the Anthropocentric Problem," *Journal of Philosophy* 82, No. 6 (1985): 281–303.

Ayer, A. J. *The Foundations of Empirical Knowledge.* New York: St. Martins Press, 1962.

Beck, Jacob. *Surface Color Perception.* Ithaca, NY: Cornell University Press, 1972.

Bennett, Jonathan. "Substance, Reality, and Primary Qualities," in *Locke and Berkeley*, Edited by C. B. Martin and D. M. Armstrong, 1968 , pp. 86–124.

Bennett, Jonathan. *Locke, Berkeley, Hume: Central Themes*. Oxford: Clarendon Press, 1971.

Berkeley, George. *A Treatise Concerning the Principles of Human Knowledge*. Indianapolis: Hackett, 1982.

Berkeley, George. *Three Dialogues between Hylas and Philonous*. Indianapolis: Hackett, 1979.

Berlin, Brent, and Kay, Paul. *Basic Color Terms: Their Universality and Evolution*. Berkeley, CA: University of California Press, 1969.

Boring, Edwin G. *Sensation and Perception in the History of Experimental Psychology*. New York: Appleton-Century-Crofts, 1942.

Boyle, Robert. "The origin of forms and qualities according to the corpuscular philosophy," in *Selected Philosophical Papers of Robert Boyle*, Edited by M. A. Stewart, 1666 , pp. 1–97.

Boynton, Robert M. *Human Color Vision*. New York: Holt, Rinehart and Winston, 1979.

Brainard, David H., and Wandell, Brian A. "An Analysis of the Retinex Theory of Color Vision," *J. Opt. Soc. Am. A* 3 (1986): 1651–1661.

Brown, Robert, and Rollins, C. D. *Contemporary Philosophy in Australia*. New York: Humanities Press, 1969.

Campbell, Keith. "The implications of Land's theory of colour vision," in *Logic, Methodology, and Philosophy of Science: Vol. 6*, Edited by L. J. Cohen, 1982 , pp. 541–553.

Campbell, Keith. "Colours," in *Contemporary Philosopy in Australia*, Edited by R. Brown and C. D. Rollins, 1969, pp. 132–157.

Claiborne, Craig. *The New York Times Menu Cook Book*. New York: Harper & Row, 1966.

Cohen, Robert S., and Elkana Yehuda, eds. *Hermann von Helmholtz: Epistemological Writings*. Boston: D. Reidel, 1977.

Cohen, L. J., ed. *Logic, Methodology, and Philosophy of Science: Vol. 6*. Amsterdam: North-Holland, 1982.

Drake, Stillman. *Discoveries and Opinions of Galileo*. Garden City, New York: Doubleday & Company, Inc., 1957.

Goethe, Wolfgang. *Goethe's Theory of Colours.* London: Frank Cass & Co. Ltd., 1967.

Goodman, Nelson. *The Structure of Appearance.* Boston: D. Reidel, 1977.

Grandy, Richard E. "Red, white and blue? Stars and stripes? A modern inquiry into the physical reality of colors," unpublished ms.

Guerlac, Henry. "Can there be colors in the dark? Physical color theory before Newton," *Jour. Hist. Ideas* 47, No. 1 (1986): 3–20.

Hardin, C. L. "A New Look at Color," *Am. Phil. Quart.* 21, No. 2 (1984): 125–133.

Hardin, C. L. "Are 'Scientific' Objects Coloured?" *Mind* 93 (1984): 491–500.

Hardin, Clyde L. "Colors, Normal Observers, and Standard Conditions," *J. Phil.* 53, No. 12 (1983): 806–813.

Helson, Harry. "Fundamental Problems in Color Vision. I. The Principle Governing Changes in Hue, Saturation, and Lightness of Non–Selective Samples in Chromatic Illumination," *J. Exp. Psych.* 23, No. 5 (1938): 439–476.

Helson, Harry. "Some Factors and Implications of Color Constancy," *J. Opt. Soc. Am.* 33, No. 10 (1943): 555–567.

Herrnstein, Richard J., and Boring, Edwin G. *A Source Book in the History of Psychology.* Cambridge, MA: Harvard University Press, 1965.

Hume, David. *Essays: Moral, Political and Literary.* Indianapolis: Liberty Classics, 1985.

Hurvich, Leo M. *Color Vison.* Sunderland, MA: Sinauer Associates Inc., 1981.

Jackson, Frank. *Perception.* Cambridge: Cambridge University Press, 1977

Jacobs, Gerald H. *Comparative Color Vision.* New York: Academic Press, 1981.

Johnson, W. E. *Logic (Part I).* London: Cambridge Unversity Press, 1921.

Judd, Deane B. "Hue, saturation and lightness of surface colors with chromatic illumination," *J. Opt. Soc. Am.* 30 (1940): 2–32.

Judd, Deane B., and Wyszecki, Gunter. *Color in Business, Science and Industry.* New York: John Wiley & Sons, 1975.

Katz, David. *The World of Colour*. London: Kegan Paul, Trench, Trubner & Co. Ltd., 1935.

Kelly, Kenneth L., and Judd, Deane B. *The ISCC–NBS Method of Designating Colors and A Dictionary of Color Names*. National Bureau of Standards, 1955.

Kirk, G. S., and Raven, J. E., and Schofield, M. *The Presocratic Philosophers*. Cambridge: Cambridge University Press, 1983.

Kripke, Saul A. *Naming and Necessity*. Cambridge, MA: Harvard University Press, 1980.

Land, Edwin H. "The retinex theory of color vision," *Sci. Am.* 237, No. 6 (1977): 108–128.

Land, Edwin H. "Recent advances in retinex theory and some implications for cortical computations: Color vision and the natural image," *Proc. Natl. Acad. Sci. USA* 80 (1983): 5163–5169.

Land, Edwin H., and McCann, John J. "Lightness and Retinex theory," *J. Opt. Soc. Am.* 61, No. 1 (1971): 1–11.

Lewis, C. I. *Mind and the World Order*. New York: Dover Publications, Inc., 1929.

Locke, John. *An Essay concerning Human Understanding*. New York: Oxford University Press, 1975.

MacAdam, D. L. *Color Measurement*. Berlin: Springer–Verlag, 1985.

Mackie, J. L. *Problems From Locke*. Oxford: Clarendon Press, 1976.

Maerz, A., and Paul, M. Rea. *A Dictionary of Color*. New York: McGraw-Hill Book Co., Inc., 1950.

Maloney, Laurence T. *Computational Approaches to Color Constancy*. Doctoral dissertation, Stanford University, 1984.

Maloney, Laurence T., and Wandell, Brian A. "Color constancy: a method for recovering surface spectral reflectance," *J. Opt. Soc. Am. A* 3, No. 1 (1986): 29–33.

Marc–Wogau, Konrad. "The Argument from Illusion and Berkeley's Idealism," in *Locke and Berkeley*, Edited by C. B. Martin and D. M. Armstrong, 1968 , pp. 340–352.

Martin, C. B., and Armstrong, D. M., eds. *Locke and Berkeley*. Notre Dame, Ind.: University of Notre Dame Press, 1968.

Maund, J. B. "Colour—A Case for Conceptual Fission," *Austral. Journ. Phil.* 59, No. 3 (1981): 308–322.

McCann, John J., and Houston, Karen L. "Calculating color sensations from arrays of physical stimuli," *IEEE Trans., Systems, Man, and Cybernetics* SMC-13, No. 5 (1983): 1000–1007.

McCann, John J., and McKee, Suzanne P. , and Taylor, Thomas H. "Quantitative studies in retinex theory: A comparison between theoretical predictions and observer responses to the 'Color Mondrian' experiments," *Vision Res.* 16 (1976): 445–458.

McGinn, Colin. *The Subjective View.* Oxford: Clarendon Press, 1983.

Nassau, Kurt. *The Physics and Chemistry of Color.* New York: John Wiley & Sons, 1983.

Newton, Isaac. *Opticks.* New York: Dover Publications, Inc., 1979.

Newton, Isaac. "Optica," in *The Optical Papers of Isaac Newton: Vol. 1, The Optical Lectures, 1670–1672,* Edited by Alan E. Shapiro, 1984 , pp. 280–604.

Newton, Isaac. "Lectiones opticæ," in *The Optical Papers of Isaac Newton: Vol. 1, The Optical Lectures, 1670–1672,* Edited by Alan E. Shapiro, 1984 , pp. 46–279.

Ostrovsky, Yu. I. *Holography and Its Application.* Moscow: Mir Publishers, 1977.

Peacocke, Christopher. *Sense and Content.* Oxford: Clarendon Press, 1983.

Peacocke, Christopher. "Colour concepts and colour experience," *Synthese* 58 (1984): 365–381.

Price, H. H. *Perception.* London: Methuen, 1950.

Rock, Irvin. *The Nature of Perceptual Adaptation.* New York: Basic Books, 1966.

Russell, Bertrand. *Human Knowledge: Its Scope and Limits.* New York: Simon and Schuster, 1948.

Russell, Bertrand. *The Problems of Philosophy.* Oxford: Oxford University Press, 1912.

Sabra, A. I. *Theories of Light from Descartes to Newton.* New York: Cambridge University Press, 1981.

Savage, C. Wade. *Perception and Cognition: Issues in the Foundations of Psychology.* Minneapolis: University of Minnesota Press, 1978.

Shapiro, Alan E., ed. *The Optical Papers of Isaac Newton: Vol. 1, The Optical Lectures, 1670–1672.* New York: Cambridge University Press, 1984.

Shepard, Roger N. "On the Status of 'Direct' Psychophysical Measurement," in *Perception and Cognition: Issues in the Foundations of Psychology*, Edited by L. Wade Savage, 1978 , pp. 441–490.

Sherman, Paul D. *Colour Vision in the Nineteenth Century*. Bristol: Adam Hilger Ltd., 1981.

Shoemaker, Sydney. "Review of Colin Mcginn: *The Subjective View*," *Journal of Philosophy* 83, No. 7 (1986): 407–413.

Sloan, Louise L., and Wallach, Lorraine. "A case of unilateral deuteranopia," *J. Opt. Soc. Am.* 38, No. 6 (1948): 502–509.

Smart, J. J. C. "Colours," *Philosophy* 36 (1961): 128–141.

Smart, J. J. C. *Philosophy and Scientific Realism*. London: Routledge & Kegan Paul, 1963.

Smart, J. J. C. "On some criticisms of a physicalist theory of colors," in *Philosophical Aspect of the Mind–Body Problem*, Edited by Chung–ying Cheng, 1975 , pp. 54–63.

Stewart, M. A. *Selected Philosophical Papers of Robert Boyle*. New York: Barnes & Noble Books, 1979.

Teevan, Richard C., and Birney, Robert C. *Color Vision: An Enduring Problem in Psychology*. Princeton, NJ: D. Van Nostrand Co., 1961.

von Helmholtz, Hermann. "The Facts in Perception," in *Hermann von Helmholtz: Epistemological Writings*, Edited by Robert S. Cohen and Yehuda Elkana, 1977 , pp. 115–185.

Wandell, Brian A. "The Synthesis and Analysis of Color Images." Ames Research Center: NASA Technical Memorandum 86844, 1985.

Westphal, Jonathan. "The Complexity of Quality," *Philosophy* 59 (1984): 457–471.

Wittgenstein, Ludwig. *Remarks on Colour*. Los Angeles, CA: University of California Press, 1977.

Worthey, James A. "Limitations of color constancy," *J. Opt. Soc. Am. A* 2, No. 7 (1985): 1014–1026.

Wright, W. D. *The Rays are not Coloured*. New York: American Elsevier , 1967.

Zeki, Semir. "Colour Coding in the Cerebral Cortex: The Responses of Wavelength–Selective and Colour–Coded Cells in Monkey Visual Cortex to Changes in Wavelength Composition," *Neuroscience* 9, No. 4 (1983): 767–781.

Zeki, Semir. "The representation of colours in the cerebral cortex," *Nature* 284, No. 3 (1980): 412–418.

Zeki, Semir. "Colour coding in the cerebral cortex: The reaction of cells in monkey visual cortex to wavelengths and colours," *Neuroscience* 9, No. 4 (1983): 741–765.

CSLI Publications

Reports

The following titles have been published in the CSLI Reports series. These reports may be obtained from CSLI Publications, Ventura Hall, Stanford University, Stanford, CA 94305.

The Situation in Logic–I. Jon Barwise. CSLI–84–2. ($2.00)

Coordination and How to Distinguish Categories. Ivan Sag, Gerald Gazdar, Thomas Wasow, and Steven Weisler. CSLI–84–3. ($3.50)

Belief and Incompleteness. Kurt Konolige. CSLI–84–4. ($4.50)

Equality, Types, Modules and Generics for Logic Programming. Joseph Goguen and José Meseguer. CSLI–84–5. ($2.50)

Lessons from Bolzano. Johan van Benthem. CSLI–84–6. ($1.50)

Self-propagating Search: A Unified Theory of Memory. Pentti Kanerva. CSLI–84–7. ($9.00)

Reflection and Semantics in LISP. Brian Cantwell Smith. CSLI–84–8. ($2.50)

The Implementation of Procedurally Reflective Languages. Jim des Rivières and Brian Cantwell Smith. CSLI–84–9. ($3.00)

Parameterized Programming. Joseph Goguen. CSLI–84–10. ($3.50)

Morphological Constraints on Scandinavian Tone Accent. Meg Withgott and Per-Kristian Halvorsen. CSLI–84–11. ($2.50)

Partiality and Nonmonotonicity in Classical Logic. Johan van Benthem. CSLI–84–12. ($2.00)

Shifting Situations and Shaken Attitudes. Jon Barwise and John Perry. CSLI–84–13. ($4.50)

Aspectual Classes in Situation Semantics. Robin Cooper. CSLI–85–14-C. ($4.00)

Completeness of Many-Sorted Equational Logic. Joseph Goguen and José Meseguer. CSLI–84–15. ($2.50)

Moving the Semantic Fulcrum. Terry Winograd. CSLI–84–17. ($1.50)

On the Mathematical Properties of Linguistic Theories. C. Raymond Perrault. CSLI–84–18. ($3.00)

A Simple and Efficient Implementation of Higher-order Functions in LISP. Michael P. Georgeff and Stephen F.Bodnar. CSLI–84–19. ($4.50)

On the Axiomatization of "if-then-else". Irène Guessarian and José Meseguer. CSLI–85–20. ($3.00)

The Situation in Logic–II: Conditionals and Conditional Information. Jon Barwise. CSLI–84–21. ($3.00)

Principles of OBJ2. Kokichi Futatsugi, Joseph A. Goguen, Jean-Pierre Jouannaud, and José Meseguer. CSLI–85–22. ($2.00)

Querying Logical Databases. Moshe Vardi. CSLI–85–23. ($1.50)

Computationally Relevant Properties of Natural Languages and Their Grammar. Gerald Gazdar and Geoff Pullum. CSLI–85–24. ($3.50)

An Internal Semantics for Modal Logic: Preliminary Report. Ronald Fagin and Moshe Vardi. CSLI–85–25. ($2.00)

The Situation in Logic–III: Situations, Sets and the Axiom of Foundation. Jon Barwise. CSLI–85–26. ($2.50)

Semantic Automata. Johan van Benthem. CSLI–85–27. ($2.50)

Restrictive and Non-Restrictive Modification. Peter Sells. CSLI–85–28. ($3.00)

144

Institutions: Abstract Model Theory for Computer Science. J. A. Goguen and R. M. Burstall. CSLI–85–30. ($4.50)

A Formal Theory of Knowledge and Action. Robert C. Moore. CSLI–85–31. ($5.50)

Finite State Morphology: A Review of Koskenniemi (1983). Gerald Gazdar. CSLI–85–32. ($1.50)

The Role of Logic in Artificial Intelligence. Robert C. Moore. CSLI–85–33. ($2.00)

Applicability of Indexed Grammars to Natural Languages. Gerald Gazdar. CSLI–85–34. ($2.00)

Commonsense Summer: Final Report. Jerry R. Hobbs, et al.. CSLI–85–35. ($12.00)

Limits of Correctness in Computers. Brian Cantwell Smith. CSLI–85–36. ($2.50)

On the Coherence and Structure of Discourse. Jerry R. Hobbs. CSLI–85–37. ($3.00)

The Coherence of Incoherent Discourse. Jerry R. Hobbs and Michael H. Agar. CSLI–85–38. ($2.50)

The Structures of Discourse Structure. Barbara Grosz and Candace L. Sidner. CSLI–85–39. ($4.50)

A Complete Type-free, Second-order Logic and its Philosophical Foundations. Christopher Menzel. CSLI–86–40. ($4.50)

Possible-world Semantics for Auto-epistemic Logic. Robert C. Moore. CSLI–85–41. ($2.00)

Deduction with Many-Sorted Rewrite. José Meseguer and Joseph A. Goguen. CSLI–85–42. ($1.50)

On Some Formal Properties of Metarules. Hans Uszkoreit and Stanley Peters. CSLI–85–43. ($1.50)

Language, Mind, and Information. John Perry. CSLI–85–44. ($2.00)

Constraints on Order. Hans Uszkoreit. CSLI–86–46. ($3.00)

Linear Precedence in Discontinuous Constituents: Complex Fronting in German. Hans Uszkoreit. CSLI–86–47. ($2.50)

A Compilation of Papers on Unification-Based Grammar Formalisms, Parts I and II. Stuart M. Shieber, Fernando C.N. Pereira, Lauri Karttunen, and Martin Kay. CSLI–86–48. ($4.00)

An Algorithm for Generating Quantifier Scopings. Jerry R. Hobbs and Stuart M. Shieber. CSLI–86–49. ($2.50)

Verbs of Change, Causation, and Time. Dorit Abusch. CSLI–86–50. ($2.00)

Noun-Phrase Interpretation. Mats Rooth. CSLI–86–51. ($2.50)

Noun Phrases, Generalized Quantifiers and Anaphora. Jon Barwise. CSLI–86–52. ($2.50)

Circumstantial Attitudes and Benevolent Cognition. John Perry. CSLI–86–53. ($1.50)

A Study in the Foundations of Programming Methodology: Specifications, Institutions, Charters and Parchments. Joseph A. Goguen and R. M. Burstall. CSLI–86–54. ($2.50)

Quantifiers in Formal and Natural Languages. Dag Westerståhl. CSLI–86–55. ($7.50)

Intentionality, Information, and Matter. Ivan Blair. CSLI–86–56. ($3.00)

Graphs and Grammars. William Marsh. CSLI–86–57. ($2.00)

Computer Aids for Comparative Dictionaries. Mark Johnson. CSLI–86–58. ($2.00)

The Relevance of Computational Linguistics. Lauri Karttunen. CSLI–86–59. ($2.50)

Grammatical Hierarchy and Linear Precedence. Ivan A. Sag. CSLI–86–60. ($3.50)

D-PATR: A Development Environment for Unification-Based Grammars. Lauri Karttunen. CSLI–86–61. ($4.00)

A Sheaf-Theoretic Model of Concurrency. Luís F. Monteiro and Fernando C. N. Pereira. CSLI–86–62. ($3.00)

A Language/Action Perspective on
the Design of Cooperative Work
Terry Winograd CSLI–87–98. (*$3.00*)

Implicature and Definite Reference
Jerry R. Hobbs CSLI–87–99. (*$1.50*)

Thinking Machines: Can There
be? Are we? Terry Winograd
CSLI–87–100. (*$2.50*)

Situation Semantics and Semantic In-
terpretation in Constraint-Based
Grammars Per-Kristian Halvorsen
CSLI–87–101. (*$1.50*)

Category Structures Gerald Gazdar,
Geoffrey K. Pullum, Robert Carpenter,
Ewan Klein, Thomas E. Hukari, Robert
D. Levine CSLI–87–102. (*$3.00*)

Cognitive Theories of Emotion Ronald
Alan Nash CSLI–87–103. (*$2.50*)

Toward an Architecture for
Resource-Bounded Agents Martha
E. Pollack, David J. Israel, and Michael
E. Bratman CSLI–87–104. (*$2.00*)

On the Relation Between Default and
Autoepistemic Logic Kurt Konolige
CSLI–87–105. (*$3.00*)

Three Responses to Situation Theory
Terry Winograd CSLI–87–106. (*$2.50*)

Subjects and Complements in HPSG
Robert Borsley CSLI–87–107. (*$2.50*)

Tools for Morphological Analysis
Mary Dalrymple, Ronald M. Kaplan,
Lauri Karttunen, Kimmo Kosken-
niemi, Sami Shaio, Michael Wescoat
CSLI–87–108. (*$10.00*)

Fourth Year Report of the Situated Language Research Program
CSLI–87–111. (*Forthcoming*)

Bare Plurals, Naked Relatives,
and Their Kin Dietmar Zaefferer
CSLI–87–112. (*Forthcoming*)

Lecture Notes

The titles in this series are distributed
by the University of Chicago Press and
may be purchased in academic or university bookstores or ordered directly
from the distributor at 5801 Ellis Avenue, Chicago, Illinois 60637.

A Manual of Intensional Logic. Johan van
Benthem. Lecture Notes No. 1.

Emotion and Focus. Helen Fay Nissen-
baum. Lecture Notes No. 2.

*Lectures on Contemporary Syntactic The-
ories.* Peter Sells with a Postscript by
Thomas Wasow. Lecture Notes No. 3.

*An Introduction to Unification-Based
Approaches to Grammar.* Stuart M.
Shieber. Lecture Notes No. 4.

The Semantics of Destructive LISP. Ian
A. Mason. Lecture Notes No. 5.

An Essay on Facts. Kenneth Russell Ol-
son. Lecture Notes No. 6.

Logics of Time and Computation. Robert
Goldblatt. Lecture Notes No. 7.

*Word Order and Constituent Structure
in German.* Hans Uszkoreit. Lecture
Notes No. 8.

Prolog and Natural-Language Analysis.
Fernando C.N. Pereira and Stuart M.
Shieber. Lecture Notes No. 10.

*Working Papers in Grammatical Theory
and Discourse: Interactions of Morphol-
ogy, Syntax, and Discourse.* M. Iida,
S. Wechsler, and D. Zec (eds.), with an
Introduction by Joan Bresnan. Lecture
Notes No. 11.

*Natural Language Processing in the 1980s:
A Bibliography* Gerald Gazdar, Alex
Franz, Karen Osborne, and Roger
Evans. Lecture Notes No. 12.

*Information-Based Syntax and Semantics:
Volume 1 Fundamentals.* Carl Pollard
and Ivan Sag. Lecture Notes No. 13.